A Long Bridge Over Deep Waters

by

JAMES STILL

(Large-cast version)

Commissioned by Cornerstone Theater Company

for the Faith-Based Theater Cycle

Dramatic Publishing

Woodstock, Illinois • England • Australia • New Zealand

*** NOTICE ***

©MMVI by
JAMES STILL
Printed in the United States of America
All Rights Reserved
(A LONG BRIDGE OVER DEEP WATERS
- Large-cast version)

For inquiries concerning all other rights, contact:
Judy Boals, Inc., 307 W. 38th St., #812,
New York NY 10018 - Phone: (212) 500-1424 - Fax: (212) 500-1426

ISBN: 1-58342-362-1

IMPORTANT BILLING AND CREDIT REQUIREMENTS

All producers of the Play must give credit to the Author of the Play in all programs distributed in connection with performances of the Play and in all instances in which the title of the Play appears for purposes of advertising, publicizing or otherwise exploiting the Play and/or a production. The name of the Author must also appear on a separate line, on which no other name appears, immediately following the title, and must appear in size of type not less than fifty percent the size of the title type. Biographical information on the Author, if included in the playbook, may be used in all programs. In all programs this notice must appear:

"Produced by special arrangement with
DRAMATIC PUBLISHING COMPANY of Woodstock, Illinois"

* * * *

All producers of the Play must include the following acknowledgment on the title page of all programs distributed in connection with performances of the Play and on all advertising and promotional materials:

"This play was originally commissioned and produced by
Cornerstone Theater Company, Los Angeles, California."

"All the world is just a narrow bridge. And the most important thing is not to be afraid."

— Rebbe Nachman of Breslov

* * * *

Help!
Theatre, come to my rescue!
I am asleep. Wake me
I am lost in the dark, guide me, at least towards a candle
I am lazy, shame me
I am tired, raise me up
I am indifferent, strike me
I remain indifferent, beat me up
I am afraid, encourage me
I am ignorant, teach me
I am monstrous, make me human
I am pretentious, make me die of laughter
I am cynical, take me down a peg
I am foolish, transform me
I am wicked, punish me
I am dominating and cruel, fight against me
I am pedantic, make fun of me
I am vulgar, elevate me
I am mute, untie my tongue
I no longer dream, call me a coward or a fool
I have forgotten, throw Memory in my face
I feel old and stale, make the Child in me leap up
I am heavy, give me Music
I am sad, bring me Joy
I am deaf, make Pain shriek like a storm
I am agitated, let Wisdom rise within me
I am weak, kindle Friendship
I am blind, summon all the Lights
I am dominated by Ugliness, bring in conquering Beauty
I have been recruited by Hatred, unleash all the forces of Love

— Ariane Mnouchkine, Theatre du Soleil

A Long Bridge Over Deep Water was originally commissioned by Cornerstone Theater Company, Los Angeles, California, Bill Rauch, artistic director, Shay Wafer, managing director. Cornerstone presented the world premiere of the play at the John Anson Ford Amphitheatre on June 4, 2005. Direction was by Bill Rauch, choreography by Otis Sallid, scenic design by Christopher Acebo, costume design by Lynn Jeffries, lighting design by Geoff Korf, music and sound by Paul James Prendergast, video direction by Yule Caise and dramaturgy by Scott Horstein. The stage managers were Michelle Blair and Anna Belle Gilbert. The cast was:

Loraine Shields, Andrew Cohen, Emily Goulding, Jennie Hahn, Naveed Merchant, Martin Alcala, Greg Cruz, Manuel Sanchez, DeLanna Studi, Sally Ben-Tal, George "Jiddu" Haddad, Natch Narasimhan, Toufiq Tulsiram, Nancy Yee, Leonard Wu, Mark Strunin, Debra Piver, Michele Derosa, Mark Brust, Joseph Gorelik, Dorothy James, Sofia Azizi, Jeff Sugarman, Adina Porter, JoAnn Charles Smith, George Gant, Virdell Twine, Diana Elizabeth Jordan, Pierre Chambers, Dora Hardie, Fred Fluker, Myron Jackson, Peter Howard, Michael Phillip Edwards, Page Leong, Shishir Kurup, K.T. Thangavelu, Sabrinath Touzene, Yogananda Touzene, Badrinath Touzene, Guiness the Dog, Elham Jazab, Ibrahim Saba, Olga Gorelik, Gezel Remy, Nathaniel Justiniano, Abdulla Al-Muntheri, Bennett Schneider, Berkeley Sanjay, Piyush Ved, Geeta Malik, Meena Serendib, Natasha Atalla, Lisa Robins, Ramy Eletreby, Ebonie Hubbard, Stephanie Nunez, Jonathan Del Arco.

AUTHOR'S NOTES

Days after *A Long Bridge Over Deep Waters* closed in Los Angeles, I was in a cab going to the airport. My cab driver, in the course of about two minutes, told me that he was 66 years old, was born in India, was a Methodist, was raised in London, and had been in Los Angeles for forty years. And he practices the Kabbalah. It was a very strangely typical conversation that I had had in one form or another during the four years of working on *Long Bridge*. Somehow, people knew that I needed to know.

The most striking thing my cab driver said, though, was when he asked me where I was going, and I said I was going to Seattle to a theater conference. He listened and then said, "Theater is a place where you can see God." He looked at me in the rearview mirror as he said that, to see what I was going to say. And I leaned forward, and he continued to talk.

That was pretty much my experience of working on this play, sitting in story circles with people of many different faiths, where people would talk and I would find myself leaning forward.

When artistic director Bill Rauch asked me to write the final play in Cornerstone Theater Company's multi-year Faith-Based Theater Cycle, I did not say yes immediately. One reason was because everyone at the time was referring to it as "The Impossible Play." What it involved was ultimately bringing together all of the communities of faith that had been working with Cornerstone, that I would be writing a play that featured Catholic immigrants, African-American Christians, Buddhists, Baha'is, Hindus, Muslims and LGBT people of faith. So I didn't say yes. I thought about it. I eventually did say yes, and then I did something crazy, which was to add two more communities of faith, which were the Tongva/Gabrielino Native American community (the original people of the Los Angeles basin), and the Atheist/

6

non-believers. So now I was dealing with ten communities of faith.

I should also point out that the first play I saw in the cycle was in the Festival of Faith, which was at New Horizons, the Islam school. It was a couple of weeks after 9/11 and what struck me was that I was going to this private Islam school, there was a lot of security there, and we had to show our picture I.D. to get in to see the plays.

For several years then, I shadowed all of the plays in the cycle. I attended some rehearsals, saw all the plays in performance, and went to community and company meetings that pertained to the cycle. I also began hosting my own series of what we called story circles. There are many names for this, many of you out there do this kind of work, oral histories, interviews, whatever you want to call it. But in the Cornerstone tradition it was literally people sitting around in a circle, telling their stories, primarily around issues of faith. Those gatherings happened often at the Cornerstone offices in downtown Los Angeles and other times in places of worship. There were anywhere from two to twenty-five people in those story circles. They took about two hours usually, and I did dozens and dozens and dozens of those with thousands of hours of audiotapes.

Some of the story circles were with specific communities of faith, others were interfaith. One was a story circle of converts. One was a story circle with women only, and me. One was a story circle about relationship to prayer, about when and how people talk to God. Another story circle was centered around food from their favorite religious holidays, and the family stories that were attached to those rituals.

All of that time I was committed to not writing the play ahead of time, to not having an agenda, to not figuring it all out neatly and then going through the motions, but instead trying to stay as completely open as I could to the process, and to absorb, as deeply as I could, the stories that my community was telling me. It was for me the ultimate act of faith.

While I wasn't writing the play, I was, hysterically and in a very big panic, thinking about the structure of the play. That was the biggest challenge to me. How was I going to bring ten communities of faith together in something that would not feel like "We Are the World"?

At some point I revisited Schnitzler's "La Ronde." Director Bill Rauch and I got very excited about the idea of that structure, and how that would help us theatrically tell the story of how faith both unites and divides us, which was a credo that was on all of the Cornerstone literature around the cycle, and one that I took very seriously.

Once we decided on that structure, then it came to the big question of, what order? In "La Ronde" the play goes from one two-person scene to another two-person scene and something is passed along. How would I determine the order of these ten communities of faith in my play? Bill and I played many games with ourselves, little pieces of paper, putting them in all different combinations, lists. Some of those structures were more provocative. Some of them had better flow. Some of them I immediately could imagine what the scenes were about. Others, I had no idea. So I found myself getting more and more depressed, because I felt like we had a structure but I had no idea how to do it.

Finally, I decided that we needed to find an order that was mathematical, in a way that was almost defensible. We decided on a structure that would go in historical order. We went to the Los Angeles census, we studied and cited major events, beginning with the Tongva Native Americans, obviously, the founding of the first Jewish temple, a visit to Los Angeles from a famous Baha'i leader, all the way through to the founding of the Metropolitan community church in 1968, which was of course the LGBT community.

With the order and structure in place, I began a series of community dialogues where I brought together two communities at a time, usually four people (purposefully kept very small) and I sat on the side and said, "For ninety minutes, we're going to have a conversation and the only rule is, you get to ask these people from another faith anything you've ever wanted to know about that other faith." The only other ground rule was the person being asked had the right to say, "I really don't want to talk about that." It's worth noting that no one ever refused to respond to the other's questions.

Eventually I went off and wrote the first draft of *A Long Bridge Over Deep Waters*. I had two things taped up on my wall as I was writing it. One said, "How does faith both unite and divide us?" And the other said, "You can't please everyone." I later changed that to read, "You can't please anyone." It was actually quite liberating. My goal was to write a play that was an authentic artistic response to what I had personally experienced as a person in the very privileged position of getting to hear people talk honestly, openly, painfully about their struggles with faith. That response is this play. Without a doubt it is the most challenging and most difficult play I've ever tried to write. And without a doubt, it was one of the richest and most surprising experiences in my life.

One final anecdote. During the run of *Long Bridge* in Los Angeles, a woman came up to me and told me that she had seen the play the previous week and was back to see it again. She went on to tell me that for years she had stopped dreaming at night, stopped remembering her dreams. But every night since she had seen *Long Bridge*—she had had amazing dreams and had remembered them.

For me, her experience helped me remember one of the many reasons I had been drawn to theater in the first place. Theater is a place where you can remember your dreams.

— James Still

9

A Long Bridge Over Deep Waters

A Play in Two Acts
13 actors minimum.
Can be cast with as many as 50+ actors.

CHARACTERS

PROLOGUE:
Mrs. Stevenson
Mrs. Stevenson's Dear Friends *(NOTE: Four actors were used in the original production; this should be adjusted to accommodate your production.)*

   Cyril
   Amilia
   Olive
   Yogananda

Pilgrimage Players *(NOTE: Entire cast on stage from beginning and also play other roles in the various scenes.)*
Native American Elder
Native American Percussionist *(NOTE: This was specific to the original production.)*
Native American Flute Player *(NOTE: This was specific to the original production.)*

SCENE ONE: THE LANGUAGE LESSON
Julia
Mrs. Stepankova
Mr. Shammas
Mr. Diggavi
Mr. Masih
Mrs. Nhim
Tevy

SCENE TWO: WINTER/SPRING
Ruth

Avrum (Ruth's father) *(NOTE: This was specific to the original production.)*

Rose (Ruth's mother) *(NOTE: This was specific to the original production.)*

Miriam (Ruth's grandma) *(NOTE: This was specific to the original production.)*

Sid (Ruth's uncle) *(NOTE: This was specific to the original production.)*

David (Ruth's little brother) *(NOTE: This was specific to the original production.)*

Ruth as a little girl *(NOTE: This was specific to the original production.)*

Tevy

SCENE THREE: A HEART IS WHERE THE HOME IS
Alan

Regina

Tee-Tee

Regina's Dad

Regina's Mom

Regina's Sister

Regina's Co-Worker

Regina's Friend

Regina's Neighbor

Pastor Quentin

SCENE FOUR: HOUSTON: WE HAVE A PROBLEM
Anderson

Redwood

Houston Control (Voice Only)

SCENE FIVE: LOCATION, LOCATION, LOCATION
Diana
Ajay
Lisa
Oldest Son
Middle Son
Youngest Son
The Dog

SCENE SIX: THERE MUST BE SOME MISTAKE
Ajay
Mother
Father
Sister-in-Law
Omeed
ShahAb

SCENE SEVEN: DECLARATION
Storyteller
Lord Shiva
Bhasmasura
Vishnu/Mohini
Foley Artist
Omeed
ShahAb

SCENE EIGHT: SPANISH 101 FOR TWO HINDUS AND A MUSLIM"
Shama
Jayanti
Sangita
Tameem

SCENE NINE: THE SECRET
Connie
Tameem
Joy
Michelle

SCENE TEN: JESUS OF LOS ANGELES
Jesus
Jula

TIME: Now.

PLACE: Los Angeles.

ACT ONE

Inside the John Anson Ford Theatre. On stage: 48 empty chairs. Our only company is each other.

OFF TO THE SIDE: *Six chairs around a big dining table.*

20 MINUTES BEFORE CURTAIN: *MRS. STEVENSON and SEVERAL OF HER DEAR FRIENDS sit at the dining table enjoying cake and lemonade. The PILGRIM-AGE PLAYERS begin to trickle on stage. They are actors, all distinctly dressed in heavy Biblical garb. One by one, in small groups, gradually they enter, watching the audience, and sit in the 48 chairs.*

AT PLACES: *All 48 chairs are filled with the PILGRIM-AGE PLAYERS. They look out at the audience.*

PROLOGUE

MRS. STEVENSON takes her rightful place behind a standing microphone in a pool of light. It is a moment for her to savor. MRS. STEVENSON is dressed beautifully in early 1920s attire, not a hair out of place. Something about her says "rich and important." She holds a big old manuscript. If she opens it, you know that dust will fly, that passion and memories are trapped in those pages. The on-stage PILGRIMAGE PLAYERS applaud MRS. STEVENSON.

MRS. STEVENSON *(to her PLAYERS)*. Thank you. Thank you, dears. *(To the audience.)* Good evening. And welcome to the Pilgrimage Theatre. *(Clearing her throat.)* My name is Mrs. Christine Wetherill Stevenson, and I was the original owner of this theater. When I arrived in Hollywood in 1917, I wanted to bring culture to the community by presenting religious plays. My first endeavor was to produce an outdoor drama called *Light of Asia*—which featured the character of Buddha. That experience led me to seek stories of the other great masters known to the world—my plan was to dramatize all of them. I had so many plans! But I'm getting ahead of myself. *(Clears her throat.)* I'm a little nervous. *(Looking out at the audience.)* My name is Mrs. Christine Wetherill Stevenson— *(Beat.)* And I've been dead for over eighty years… *(She stops—looking around the space.)* I can't seem to leave this place, this theater. It's like my home, my church. *(She pauses, regaining her composure.)* Before I came to Los Angeles I had never even opened a Bible. But in 1920 I stood at the corner of Highland Avenue and Hollywood Boulevard, gazing northward at the Cahuenga Pass… *(Remembering.)* It seemed to me to be the most spiritual place in all of Los Angeles. In that moment I knew that this was the perfect setting for a play I was writing about the life of the Christ called *The Pilgrimage Play*. So I purchased this 29-acre ravine—and work soon began on building my theater which I called the Pilgrimage Theatre. *(Passion-ate:)* What a time that was! I wrote the entire play based on my own translation of the four Gospels according to the King James version of the Bible. Then I journeyed to the Holy Land and brought back authentic fabrics and props which we used in our production. I was also the director of that first production. For years my play was performed here by noted actors—dear, dear friends—many of whom you see here tonight. Ghosts. *(She looks around at her beloved PLAYERS, moved by them all over again. To us:)* Anyway dears, it's now been more than forty years since the last performance of my play—and all that time we've been waiting. Every night—me and my dear actors—we've been waiting for you. And here you are. *(Looking out at the audience, emotional.)* Dear, dear audience. *(Beat.)* Let us wait no longer. This city, this theater, this ground—cries out for this story.

(MRS. STEVENSON is re-seated with her DEAR FRIENDS at the dining table off to the side. Not only do they have a great view of the play—but the audience has a great view of them watching the play too. The microphone is struck. The PILGRIMAGE PLAYERS all take their places for the beginning of The Pilgrimage Play. *The lights change. Strange silence. Then MUSIC:)*

The Pilgrimage Play by Christine Wetherill Stevenson:

"The Voices of Judea"

PILGRIMAGE PLAYER #1. In the beginning was the Word,

PILGRIMAGE PLAYER #2. And the Word was with God,

PILGRIMAGE PLAYER #3. And the Word was God.

PILGRIMAGE PLAYER #4. And the Word was made flesh

PILGRIMAGE PLAYER #5. And dwelt among us.

PILGRIMAGE PLAYER #6. And we beheld his glory;

PILGRIMAGE PLAYER #7. The Glory as of the only

PILGRIMAGE PLAYER #8. Begotten of the Father,

PILGRIMAGE PLAYER #9. Full of Grace and Truth.

PILGRIMAGE PLAYER #10. For the law was given by Moses,

PILGRIMAGE PLAYER #11. But Grace and Truth came by

ALL PILGRIMAGE PLAYERS. Jesus Christ.

(Biblical MUSIC. We are by a river. THREE PEASANT WOMEN huddle together on the bank of the river.)

PEASANT WOMAN #1. Behold, hither cometh the well-favored harlot, Magdalene—

PEASANT WOMAN #2. With her Roman lover.

(MAGDALENE and PANDIRA enter right. MAGDALENE is in a serious mood and tries to conceal it from PANDIRA.)

PANDIRA *(jovially)*. What new madness did possess ye Magdalene to come to this desolate place?

MAGDALENE *(forcing a smile)*. A prophet hath been promised to our people, and 'tis said he frequently abides here by the river—

(We hear the SOUND OF A FLUTE. PANDIRA tries to continue:)

PANDIRA *(chuckling).* A prophet! What wouldst thou with a prophet.

(The FLUTE MUSIC continues, growing stronger. The PILGRIMAGE PLAYERS look around, confused by the sound. Obviously this isn't supposed to happen... Then upstage of the PLAYERS, there is the SOUND OF SINGING.)

TONGVA ELDER. <TONGVA SINGING>

(The PLAYERS all turn to look upstage at the hillside where a light reveals AN OLDER MAN (TONGVA ELDER. The FLUTE PLAYER continues to play from the back of the house. The TONGVA ELDER continues singing upstage in the hillside. It is the "Tongva Welcoming Song." The PILGRIMAGE PLAYERS are caught in between.)

MRS. STEVENSON *(to the TONGVAS).* Excuse me! We're doing a play down here!

(Some of the PLAYERS look to MRS. STEVENSON for some idea of what they should do. She's as confused as anyone, gestures to PANDIRA to start again, anything to get her play back on track.)

PANDIRA *(forced, jovially).* What new madness did possess ye Magdalene to come to this desolate place?

*(But the WOMAN PLAYING MAGDALENE seems mes-
merized by the flute music, looking out at the audience
toward the back of the theater. Upstage on the hillside,
the TONGVA ELDER continues singing the "Tongva
Welcoming Song." Another player—JOHN THE
BAPTIST—steps forward as if to try and jump ahead to
another part of* The Pilgrimage Play.*)*

JOHN THE BAPTIST. Prepare ye the way of the Lord,
make his path straight and all flesh shall see salvation
of—of—of—

*(But it's no use. JOHN THE BAPTIST stops, distracted,
looking back at the TONGVA ELDER who continues
singing "The Welcoming Song." The WOMAN/MAG-
DALENE is now the only one not looking back up at the
TONGVA ELDER. She remains downstage, facing the
audience. She is moving, awkwardly. It's as if her bones
are trying to remember something from long ago. She is
trying to remember the language, how to move, how to
dance... Before the song can end, the moment is inter-
rupted by the RINGING OF A CELL PHONE. The
sound is foreign to the PLAYERS, some of them might
even cover their ears. The WOMAN/MAGDALENE
searches her body/clothes for the ringing. In the process
of looking for her phone, she begins to peel off layers of
the Biblical garb. Eventually she is standing in contemporary clothes, the Biblical garb in a discarded heap at
her feet. She finally discovers a ringing cell phone in a
pocket or bag—and then has to figure out what the
phone is, then tentatively answers it.)*

JULIA *(to cell phone)*. Hello? Who? *(Realization.)* Yes, this is Julia. *(From this moment on, she is JULIA.)* Who is this? Oh, God. Yes, I did. Right. I know. OK. What day do you need me to be there? OK. I don't know, but I'll cancel stuff if I have to, I'll be there. Saturday. Yes, I know— *(Firm.)* I'll be there. OK, uh-huh. No but I can Mapquest it. Yeah I know that area—I teach at a Catholic church in Long Beach. I teach English. No—the language. ESL, right. No, it's just one class—I'm really an actress. OK. Right. Saturday. Do I need to bring anything? Right. Wait—can I ask—how many are there, how many did they find? *(Listens, then long pause.)* No—I'm still here. I'll be there. Saturday. Bye. *(JULIA hangs up her cell phone—and breaks down crying.)*

PLAYER/JOHN THE BAPTIST *(urgent)*. Mrs. Stevenson, what about the play?

OLD SHEPHERD. What about OUR play?

(They all look to MRS. STEVENSON for her wisdom. She is strangely calm, shocked, but not afraid.)

MRS. STEVENSON *(matter of fact)*. I don't know, dears.

(The space begins to change all around her. MUSIC. FIVE PILGRIMAGE PLAYERS strip away their Biblical garb and transform into 21st century SENIOR CITIZENS. [NOTE: From this point, all transitions will involve the PILGRIMAGE PLAYERS stripping away the Biblical garb, revealing contemporary clothes.]

SCENE ONE: The Language Lesson
Tongva / Catholic Immigrant

(Long Beach. A small room. Part of a Catholic church or annex. Folding chairs. A blackboard. It's musty but comfortable. Everything in the room looks like it has been donated over the years from people's homes. JULIA stands at the blackboard in front of SEVERAL IMMIGRANT SENIOR CITIZENS. She points to the phrase written on the blackboard and reads it very clearly, over-emphasizing:)

JULIA. "May I use the telephone?"

IMMIGRANT SENIORS *(repeating it aloud, slowly, in unison:)*. May—I—use—the—telephone?

JULIA. Good, good. "Have a nice day!"

IMMIGRANT SENIORS. Good—good—have—a—nice—day! *(JULIA applauds her students' success; they applaud back.)*

JULIA *(smiling, nodding)*. Perfect. Now let's try this one: "It is a sunny day in Los Angeles." Everyone:

IMMIGRANT SENIORS. "It is a sunny day in Los Angeles."

JULIA. Wonderful. Everyone is improving so much.

MRS. STEPANKOVA *(raising hand)*. What is this—"improving"?

JULIA. "Improving"—um—getting better, making progress...

(All of the SENIORS talk aloud in their own languages, translating for themselves. Then:)

IMMIGRANT SENIORS *(simultaneously/overlapping)*. Yes, yes! Im-proving!

JULIA. Yes, improving! OK. Let's try an exercise. I'll start a sentence and you can fill in the blank— *(They all look at her, confused.)* Um, fill in the blank, finish the sentence. Yes? *(The class laughs, not sure what she means, but willing to try.)* Right. Uh— "My favorite thing about Los Angeles is…" *(She looks at the class, motions for them to finish the sentence. An older Indian man [MR. DIGGAVI] raises his hand, enthusiastically.)*

MR. DIGGAVI. "Catholic church!" *(The other students all nod in agreement, pleased. A murmur of "yes's" ripples across the room.)*

JULIA. Huh. The Catholic church. Well. Sure. I guess that's—that would count. Anyone else? A favorite thing about L.A.? Palm trees? The ocean, anyone? Favorite thing?

MR. DIGGAVI. "Catholic church!"

JULIA. OK. OK. Let's try this one: "Does this bus stop near…"

MR. DIGGAVI. "Catholic church!"

JULIA. Right. How about another one. Um— "This morning I saw…?"

(An Egyptian man [MR. SHAMMAS] calmly answers:)

MR. SHAMMAS. God.

JULIA. God?

MR. SHAMMAS *(halting English)*. "This—morn-ing—I saw—God."

JULIA. You saw God?

MR. SHAMMAS *(nodding)*. This morning I saw God.

JULIA. Really?

(MR. SHAMMAS just nods calmly, smiling. Suddenly JULIA begins to cry. The IMMIGRANT SENIORS are unsure of what to do, unsure how to react to their teacher crying. They begin to talk to each other in several different languages.)

IMMIGRANT SENIORS *(simultaneously)*. <Several languages: "What is wrong with her?" "Should someone get her some water?" "Maybe she's not feeling well.">

JULIA. I'm sorry, really, I—well I had some news, some bad news, SAD news right before I came here tonight, and I'm feeling a little raw.

IMMIGRANT SENIORS *(repeating the new word)*. Raw.

MRS. STEPANKOVA *(explaining to class)*. Means uncooked—like sushi.

MR. MASIH *(confused)*. How this news make you feel like sushi?

JULIA *(laughing through tears)*. No, I don't feel like sushi. Raw—um, how do I explain it? *(She looks out at the faces of the IMMIGRANT SENIORS. They are looking at her with such compassion—it only makes JULIA begin to cry again.)*

MR. MASIH. Oh! Sushi is crying, yes?

JULIA. No, no.

MR. SHAMMAS. May I ask question? Are you Catholic?

JULIA *(thinking)*. Am I Catholic? Kind of. I mean, I was born Catholic. Part of me is definitely Catholic. I think. Am I Catholic? I don't know. I guess I'm—I'm a version.

MRS. STEPANKOVA. Like Virgin Mary!

MR. DIGGAVI. I love Virgin Mary!

JULIA. No, no! God, no, I'm not a—no. This is really hard to explain. *(JULIA thinks, starts, stops, thinks again. Then finally:)* I was born—Catholic. *(The class all nods, understanding.)* But my people are Tongva—

MR. MASIH. Tong-va.

JULIA. Tongva—yes! It's the name of my people. Native Americans. Indian. *(The SENIORS nod now, understanding.)* Tongva—it means "people of the earth."

MRS. STEPANKOVA. Earth! Here, yes?

JULIA. Yes. We were here first—HERE—in California. Hundreds of years ago—before the Spanish came—

MR. DIGGAVI. Buenos dias!

JULIA *(nodding)*. Yes, and then they converted my people to Catholicism.

MR. DIGGAVI. I love Catholic church.

JULIA. I know, I know you do. But my people—they were forced—

MR. MASIH. Forced?

JULIA. Forced—made to, they were given no choice. *(Beat.)* I am Catholic AND Tongva. I am a mix—

MRS. STEPANKOVA. Cake mix!

JULIA *(laughing)*. Yes, kind of, I'm kind of like a cake mix—many ingredients. I'm made up of all that's come before me, you know?

MRS. STEPANKOVA. Catholic and Tongva.

JULIA. Sometimes I'm both, which sometimes makes me feel like I'm neither. Sometimes it just makes me feel alone.

MR. SHAMMAS. Maybe you pray? We pray for you.

JULIA. Did you really see God this morning?

MR. SHAMMAS *(nodding)*. I see God—everywhere. Always. Don't you see God?

(JULIA looks at MR. SHAMMAS, unsure what to say. A Cambodian woman (MRS. NHIM), who has been silent throughout, raises her hand.)

JULIA. Yes, Mrs. Nhim, please.

MRS. NHIM. <Speaking quickly in Khmer for two or three sentences. Translation: "Do not worry, Teacher. No matter if you see Him—God is always with you!"> *(She suddenly stops speaking in Khmer and is quiet for a moment. Then quietly, but very determined: halting.)* I want to share my worry with you, I want—to speak the English.

JULIA. Of course, yes, please.

MRS. NHIM. Sometimes life short, sometimes long—but still short. *(Beat.)* Yes? *(Beat.)* I come from Cambodia. My family all killed by Khmer Rouge. Then—I feel so alone, I prayed to God—so I never alone again. See? God always with me. I meet my husband in camp in Thailand. We come here—to California. And God came with us. God in Thailand camp. God on boat. God in Long Beach. God—how to say this...God—here! HERE, now! I feel that. I want YOU—feel that. Teacher. Good teacher. God loves you.

JULIA. Thank you. But maybe you are the teacher and I am the student.

MRS. NHIM. You speak other words?

JULIA. No, I think I've said enough.

MRS. NHIM. I mean other, um, Englishes...?

JULIA. Other languages? LANGUAGES.

IMMIGRANT SENIORS *(repeating the word)*. Lang-gua-ges—

JULIA. Only English and Spanish.

MRS. NHIM. No Tongva?

JULIA. No. I don't speak my ancestors' language. Hardly anyone does. I need to learn.

MRS. NHIM. Maybe you take class. You be student, like us.

JULIA *(smiling)*. Maybe. Maybe. Shall we try a few more phrases before we're out of time? "Do I have to change buses?"

IMMIGRANT SENIORS. "Do I have to change buses?"

JULIA. Good! "How long will it take me to get there?"

IMMIGRANT SENIORS. "Good! How long will it take me to get there?"

(JULIA's questions start to become less rote, more genuine, more personal:)

JULIA. "Will it be a difficult journey?"

IMMIGRANT SENIORS. "Will it be a difficult journey?"

JULIA. "How will I know if I am lost?"

MRS. STEPANKOVA. Just ask people:

MR. DIGGAVI. Where is Catholic church?

MR. MASIH. No lock on God's door.

MR. SHAMMAS. Lord, make me an instrument of your peace—

IMMIGRANT SENIORS. Where there is hatred,

JULIA. Let me sow love;

IMMIGRANT SENIORS. When there is injury,

JULIA. Pardon;

IMMIGRANT SENIORS. Where there is doubt,

JULIA. Faith;

IMMIGRANT SENIORS. Where there is despair,

JULIA. Hope;

IMMIGRANT SENIORS. Where there is darkness,

JULIA. Light;

IMMIGRANT SENIORS. And where there is sadness, *(Beat.)*

JULIA. Joy. *(Everyone is quiet for a moment. Maybe God IS in the room. Hearing/saying the sacred words, JULIA absorbs the meaning. Then more words come tumbling out, like childhood:)* Grant that I may not so much seek to be consoled as to console, to be understood as to under—

(A young Asian man (TEVY) appears at the doorway. JULIA stops when she sees him.)

JULIA *(cont'd)*. Well. Mrs. Nhim's son is here. Right on time. Like always. I'll see you all next week?

(Everyone nods, waves, talking on the way out. MRS. NHIM goes to JULIA:)

MRS. NHIM. We will practice English. You—will practice seeing God.

(JULIA nods, reaches out and touches MRS. NHIM's hand. MRS. NHIM exits with TEVY. Alone, JULIA drops to her knees and tries to pray—but fails. Then:)

JULIA *(angry)*. I can't see you!

(Lights slowly fade on JULIA. In the darkness we hear the SINGING of the Jewish Sabbath prayers.)

SCENE TWO: Winter/Spring
Catholic Immigrant / Jewish

(In near darkness we hear:)

ROSE. Ruthie?
YOUNG RUTH & OLD RUTH *(together)*. Yes, Mama?
ROSE. Bring me the candles.

(A match is struck. Candlelight reveals a family at sabbath dinner: 1940. FATHER [AVRUM]; MOTHER [ROSE]; AUNT [LEAH]; UNCLE [SYD]; GRANDMA [MIRIAM]; LITTLE BROTHER [DAVID]; and 10-year-old RUTH. In another pool of light An old Jewish woman [RUTH] sits at a desk staring out a window at the memory of a long-ago Sabbath dinner. Seventy-five-year-old RUTH looks tired, frail. The lines on her face suggest a life lived, someone who has given thought to anything and everything—whether she wanted to or not. Sitting in the light, she looks like a painting.)

TEVY *(O.S.)*. Ruth? I'm back!

(The young man's voice breaks RUTH's reverie. The memory of the Sabbath dinner disappears leaving RUTH only in the present. Beverly Hills. A study filled with books, books everywhere, floor to ceiling. A big window with great California afternoon sun streaming in. RUTH

looks up just as TEVY [the young Asian man from the previous scene] enters and puts some money on the desk in front of RUTH. His energy is breezy and confident; he's completely comfortable with RUTH.)

TEVY. Here's your change. Sorry it took so long, the line at the post office was like glacier-slow. *(RUTH shrugs as if to say, "What are you going to do?")* Luckily I grabbed this book from your shelf so I had something to read— *(Playful.)* I'd read the first couple of poems before I looked to see who'd written them. It was you—

RUTH. Guilty as charged.

TEVY. Then I checked out the copyright. I can't believe you wrote them so long ago.

RUTH. You mean you can't believe I was ALIVE so long ago. That was the first thing I ever published, that collection of poems.

TEVY. I liked them. That one about your parents is awesome.

RUTH *(trying the word out)*. Awesome? *(Remembering.)* My tateh didn't think so.

TEVY. Well I liked it. It's cool, you know. The way you just sit around here all day and make up beautiful poems.

RUTH. Well, not so much now. Now I just sit here out of habit.

TEVY. Have you read all these books?

RUTH. Most of them. The ones that I haven't read, I meant to read. Time—it goes by so fast.

TEVY *(laughing)*. Time isn't fast or slow, Ruth. It's just time.

RUTH. Then I must be talking about my heartbeat. *(TEVY doesn't answer, he sits at a table/desk and opens a folder of papers. RUTH continues, good-naturedly.)* What shall we argue about today?

TEVY *(ignoring her question)*. It won't take me long to finish these letters for you. *(TEVY starts typing a letter.)* You really should get a computer.

RUTH. Why?

TEVY. So I wouldn't have to use this old—what do you call it?

RUTH. Typewriter.

TEVY. Right. Ruth—it's the 21st century. Everyone uses computers.

RUTH. Everyone? For someone who studies math and probability, you are very unconvincing.

TEVY. I wasn't trying to convince you, I was just making a suggestion. *(TEVY resumes typing. YOUNG RUTH playfully touches the typewriter.)*

RUTH *(remembering)*. I've had that typewriter since I was ten years old... *(Beat.)* What are you studying this semester? Anything interesting? Do you have to do any writing in your classes?

TEVY. Actually I'm writing a paper on this guy named Richard Swinburne.

RUTH. Never heard of him.

TEVY. He's British.

RUTH. So's the Queen of England.

TEVY. He calculated the probability of Jesus' resurrection. *(This catches RUTH off guard.)*

RUTH. Hm. *(Beat.)*

TEVY. It's ninety-seven percent—in case you want to know.

RUTH. What's ninety-seven percent?

TEVY. That Jesus rose from the dead. Richard Swinburne calculated that it's ninety-seven percent probable that Jesus actually rose from the dead.

RUTH *(dry)*. Ninety-seven percent seems very high.

TEVY. It's math, Ruth, not emotion.

RUTH. Pardon me, I thought we were talking about religion.

TEVY. We are. Well, I was. Anyway, you asked. *(They work in silence.)*

RUTH. Tevy? Am I the first Jew you've ever known?

TEVY. I don't know. Probably.

RUTH. Don't worry. We're like everyone else—only more so.

TEVY *(laughs. Beat)*. I guess you're the first one, the first—Jew—that I've ever talked to...about religion, anyway. *(Silence, working, typing.)*

RUTH. So talk!

TEVY. Can I ask you a question?

RUTH. As long as it's a good one. Remember: I'm paying you by the quality of your questions.

TEVY *(laughing)*. I missed that part. My question: why don't you believe in Jesus?

RUTH. IN Jesus?!? What I believe is that Jesus was a man, a teacher.

TEVY. But as a Jew, you don't believe that He's the savior, the son of God.

RUTH. Of course not. But I DO believe that a real man named Jesus—Yeshua—was a wandering teacher. He was a rabbi, you know.

TEVY. What do you mean?

RUTH. Oh, surely you know that Jesus was Jewish.

TEVY. I guess I knew that. *(Trying the idea out:)* Jesus was Jewish.

RUTH *(pushing forward)*. He was a rabbi—a teacher. That's what "rabbi" means—"the teacher."

TEVY. How do you explain all his miracles?

RUTH. He wasn't the only miracle worker in his day. There were others—

TEVY. Maybe. But they weren't the son of God!

RUTH. All right, let me set the record straight before you imagine me sprouting horns.

TEVY. Ruth—

RUTH. Jesus inspired people. His TEACHINGS were inspiring. He was an incredible storyteller, he knew how to make great use of the parable, he was compassionate, concerned about poverty, and he fought for social justice.

TEVY. You make him sound like a Democrat.

RUTH. Ironic, isn't it? *(Sadly.)* No, it turns out that Jesus was too much of a rebel to be a Democrat. He wanted CHANGE, that's what got him into trouble. Jesus was a revolutionary Jew, Tevy.

TEVY. So Catholicism is really a reformed branch of Judaism.

RUTH. I didn't say that—

TEVY. Which makes me Jewish. Sort of.

RUTH. Absolutely not!

TEVY. Following your logic, there was this rabbi named Jesus—

RUTH. Yeshua, in Hebrew.

TEVY. And maybe Jesus wasn't thinking about starting a new religion—

RUTH.	TEVY.
HE didn't start a new religion—	
	But he did!
	He did!
OTHER people did that— and much later.	
	But his life, his teachings, they changed the world… He was Jewish, OK. But maybe —maybe he was that MOMENT, you know? That
No, no, no!	MOMENT between two things—and maybe his teachings went BEYOND Judaism.

RUTH. Hold it right there—

TEVY. Maybe Christianity is simple evolution.

RUTH. Next you're going to say that you feel sorry for me. Suddenly I feel like the Jew who prefers surface streets to the freeway.

TEVY. Ruth—

RUTH. You have all these Christians zipping along on the 10, and when they hear that all the Jews are driving on Olympic Boulevard, the Christians say, "Well why didn't you take the freeway?"

TEVY. I didn't say that—

RUTH. It suggests that something's "wrong" with being Jewish, like we're not "with it," like the poor Jews have been left behind!

TEVY. Ruth—

RUTH. Different roads can sometimes take you to the same place, Tevy.

TEVY. I know. But you still didn't answer my question: why not believe in Jesus?

RUTH *(passionate)*. "Affirm me! Affirm the risk that I'm taking by believing what I believe!" That's what I hear you saying to me.

TEVY. I didn't mean to offend you.

RUTH. If you prick us, do we not bleed? *(Beat.)* Shakespeare.

TEVY. I bet Shakespeare believed in Jesus.

RUTH. Shakespeare believed in Shakespeare. He was an artist.

TEVY *(answering his ringing cell phone)*. Hello? *(Easily switching to another language.)* <Khmer language> Translation: "Yes, Father, I paid it. It's all taken care of, everything is fine. I'm at work now." *(Then quickly in English:)* At work, right. OK. Bye. *(TEVY hangs up the phone.)* Sorry. My dad, always calling about something. He wanted to make sure I gave the rent check to our landlord. He's very proud that we always pay on time.

RUTH. You do a lot for your parents. *(TEVY shrugs.)* You never talk about them.

TEVY. Neither do you.

RUTH. I don't live with mine. And they've been dead for many years.

TEVY. Look—here's what I know, Ruth. They don't talk about it much—about what it was like in Cambodia, about the camps in Thailand. My mother had nine sisters and all of them were killed by Pol Pot. My parents met in the camps. My father was Muslim, my mother was Buddhist. But in the camps, they both chose to be Catholic. They CHOSE it. My mother believes that's what saved them. *(Erupting with passion.)* Ruth, I love being Catholic! The more I learn, the more I'm in awe of God.

RUTH. I've never wanted to be in awe of God, I've always preferred a good argument with him.

TEVY. Sounds like a Jewish thing. *(They both laugh. Then silence. TEVY returns to typing, RUTH watches him.)*

RUTH. My parents lost most of their families in a terrible war too, Tevy. Dozens of them died in camps. *(TEVY looks up at RUTH. She nods.)* I've always wondered why those terrible experiences make some people MORE sure about their religion, and others—it just seems to rob them of any peace for the rest of their lives. I suppose that's why I've spent my life writing poems. Poetry is just music made of chaos.

TEVY. But Judaism: what do you like about IT?

RUTH. I like that it's old. I like that it's been around for a long time. It's hard. Always. But it works. That's what I like about it. *(RUTH looks out the window and sees the memory of her family.)* Do you know I've lived in Los Angeles all my life? And it's only now when I'm an old woman that I've begun to understand we have four seasons here too. Everyone thinks it's always summer. But summer doesn't last forever—even in California. No. Summer. Fall. Winter. And Spring. *(Long silence.)*

TEVY. I need to go, Ruth. I finished inputting your letters.

RUTH *(correcting him)*. TYPING! You "TYPE" letters. "Input" is not a verb.

TEVY *(laughing)*. Whatever. I'll see you on Thursday.

RUTH. Tevy—wait.

TEVY *(walks back to RUTH. He dreads this)*. Are you going to fire me?

RUTH *(holds out the book of poems that TEVY had been reading earlier)*. I'd like you to have this. It's a gift.

TEVY *(touched)*. Wow. I've never had a book by the person who actually wrote it. Thank you, Ruth. I really have to run. I promised my parents that I'd drive them to church tonight. Bye. *(RUTH waves to TEVY and he's gone. She looks around her office as if to memorize every detail. Then she sits in her chair, looks out the window. In a pool of light, TEVY opens the book and reads the inscription:)* "To Tevy:

RUTH'S MEMORY FAMILY. "Baruch atah Adonai, Elohaynu, melech ha-olam, she-hecheeyanu v'keey' manu v'heegeeyanu la-z'man ha-zeh."

RUTH. "Blessed are you, Lord, our God, king of the universe, who has kept us alive, sustained us, and enabled us to reach this season."

TEVY *(reading)*. "With admiration and affection, Ruth Abrams."

(Suddenly something catches RUTH's attention. She's seeing something, something wondrous. She's staring, in awe. Lights get brighter and brighter on RUTH'S MEMORY FAMILY. Blindingly bright. Simultaneously, the lights slowly fade on RUTH. YOUNG RUTH takes a step toward RUTH and they look at each other. And then all is black.)

SCENE THREE: "A Heart Is Where the Home Is"
Jewish / Black Faith

(South Central Los Angeles. Lights up on a white man (ALAN) in his 40s, standing outside a house. It is night. ALAN stares at the numbers hanging next to the door:

36. He reaches up and touches the "36" and is startled by the loud joyful SOUNDS OF A PARTY coming from inside the house. ALAN takes a step back. He stares at the "36," seems frozen, unable to move, unable to ring the doorbell. He finally turns away and starts to leave, then abruptly turns back, charges for the door with purpose, rings the doorbell. Impatient, he rings it again.)

TEE-TEE *(O.S.)*. I'll get it!

(Finally, the door opens—and the SOUNDS OF THE PARTY come pouring out into the street like a river. An African-American teenage girl [TEE-TEE] stands at the open door and looks at ALAN.)

TEE-TEE *(cont'd)*. Hello.

REGINA'S FATHER *(from inside the house)*. Who is it, Tee-Tee?

ALAN *(nervous)*. Hi. *(They stand looking at each other.)*

REGINA'S FATHER *(from inside the house)*. Well who is it?

(ALAN reaches in his pocket and pulls out a piece of paper that's been folded and unfolded many, many times.)

ALAN. I'm looking for a Mrs. Regina Thompson. Does she live here?

TEE-TEE. Does she know you?

ALAN. No. Not exactly.

(REGINA's FATHER [an African-American man in his 60s] comes to the door.)

REGINA'S FATHER. Can I help you?

TEE-TEE. He's come to see Mama. *(ALAN visibly reacts to TEE-TEE referring to Regina Thompson as "Mama.")*

ALAN. Mama.

REGINA'S FATHER *(suspicious)*. I'm Regina's father. Does Regina know you?

ALAN. No—she doesn't. Uh, no. I...

REGINA'S FATHER. Are you all right? You look a little pale.

ALAN. Actually, I'm a little, a little—

(Several more people come to the door, crowding around to see who's outside.)

REGINA'S FATHER. I didn't catch your name.

ALAN. Of course, I'm sorry. I'm Alan. Alan Abrams.

REGINA'S VOICE *(O.S.)*. Well who is it?

ALAN *(holding up the paper)*. I've come to see Mrs. Thompson. Regina Thompson.

(REGINA [an African-American woman in her 40s] comes to the door. She moves a little slowly, but has great life in her. She's dressed up and is holding a plate with a piece of cake.)

REGINA. I'm Regina Thompson. How can I help you?

ALAN. I'm Alan. Um. I'm Alan—Abrams. I got your letter...

REGINA. I'm sorry, I don't understand.

ALAN. Your letter—the letter that you wrote my family. I mean, the Donor Center, they forwarded your letter, and you said it would be all right to contact you, you know, if we wanted to, and I guess, you know, I guess I— should have called first. Well. This turned out to be a lot harder than I thought it was going to be.

REGINA. It was someone in your family—

ALAN *(nodding)*. My mother—

REGINA & ALAN *(simultaneously)*. Her heart. *(They look at each other. No one moves.)*

REGINA. Would you like to come inside? I still get tired from standing too long. *(ALAN doesn't move.)* Please. *(REGINA reaches out and takes ALAN's hand.)* We're having a party out back.

(REGINA leads ALAN inside. The space is suddenly filled with little white twinkle lights. We are now in RE-GINA's backyard which is alive with decorations and handmade signs. The twinkle lights are like stars in the sky. The party comes to an awkward thud: everyone looking at ALAN.)

REGINA *(cont'd)*. Everyone—this is Mr. Abrams. *(Someone helps REGINA to a chair and she sits, with great relief.)*

ALAN. I really don't mean to intrude—

REGINA. Now don't even start with that kind of talk.

TEE-TEE. We're celebrating Mama's homecoming. I did all the decorations.

REGINA'S SISTER. It's a miracle to have her home with us.

REGINA'S FRIEND. It IS a miracle.

REGINA'S MOTHER. Can we get you something to drink? Some cake?

ALAN. I'd love something to drink.

REGINA'S NEIGHBOR. Lemonade?

ALAN. Lemonade is perfect. Thank you. *(It's quiet again, a little uncomfortable.)* I feel really silly now. Barging in like this. I'm not sure why I came, not sure what I'm looking for. I guess I wanted to see you. I wanted to SEE you. Mrs. Thompson.

REGINA. Regina. *(Beat.)* I'm very sorry about your mother. I'm glad to meet you. *(REGINA's NEIGHBOR hands ALAN a glass of lemonade.)* You know, Mr. Abrams—

ALAN. Alan.

REGINA. Alan. I wasn't sure I wanted to meet you, the family. *(Beat.)* I wrote that letter because I've been having these dreams. They started right after the surgery... The kind of dreams I've never had before... I wake up, write down little sayings, words, poems— I'd never written a poem in my life—

(ALAN suddenly drops the glass of lemonade, it spills everywhere. Everyone rushes to clean it up.)

ALAN. I am so sorry.

PASTOR QUENTIN. Are you sure you're all right?

ALAN. It's just that my mother—she was a poet. *(They all look at him.)*

REGINA. She wrote poems.

ALAN. Yes. All her life. That's what she did, I mean, that's—who she was. She was a writer. Poems. Ruth Abrams. She was kind of famous.

REGINA. You must miss her.

ALAN. I do. I mean, to be honest, we didn't always have the greatest relationship. Jewish mothers and sons, you know.

TEE-TEE. Wait: Mama has a Jewish heart?

REGINA'S MOTHER. Tee-Tee.

TEE-TEE. What?

ALAN. It's all right.

REGINA. Did you sit shiva?

ALAN *(surprised)*. You know about shiva?

REGINA. I had a great-grandfather who was Jewish—

REGINA'S FATHER. Now we don't know that for sure.

REGINA. Daddy: his name was Goldberg. *(ALAN can't help but laugh.)* Great-grandpa Goldberg.

ALAN. Sounds pretty Jewish.

REGINA. Big family secret, you know. I never knew him but I'm the one who's always been interested in the family history. I thought I might learn more about him by doing a little reading about Jews— *(awkward)* about being a Jew—about the Jewish faith. Something about sitting shiva made sense to me.

ALAN. Actually, I did sit shiva for my mother. I never thought I'd do that. I'm not a very religious person, I uh, I mean I'm Jewish. But not JEWISH.

REGINA. Well we're Methodist. And I DO mean METHODIST. *(Everyone laughs.)*

ALAN. Can I ask you a personal question? *(REGINA nods.)* Do you, FEEL any different. I mean—aside from the dreams—

REGINA. And the poetry.

ALAN. Right. Amazing.

REGINA. It's hard to explain, even to myself. How it feels…maybe it's like when I was pregnant with my

kids. I felt this—LIFE—inside me. Tee-Tee there, especially. She was always moving around in there, kicking
and poking and tossing and turning. Now, I have this
new heart, your mother's heart—LIFE. Before, my own
heart—I hardly ever noticed it, felt it. I mean, when I
met my husband I know my heart was beating pretty
fast. And there have been times when I've felt God so
strongly, or knew that Jesus Christ was doing good-
ness—and I remember feeling my heart then too. Very
strongly. But most of the time, I never thought about it.
Now. This heart, I feel it all the time. It's different, the
way it beats, the intensity—

ALAN. My mother was definitely intense. And stubborn.
At first, the doctors told her she might be too old, you
know, too old to be a donor. But she refused to give up
on the idea. That's just the way she was…

TEE-TEE. Did your mother like to argue?

ALAN (smiling). Yes she did. When I was growing up she
used to pay me an allowance based on the quality of my
questions.

TEE-TEE. Then that explains why Mama argues with me
about everything now!

REGINA. Tee-Tee—

TEE-TEE. I'm just saying.

REGINA. I know what you're just saying.

REGINA'S FATHER (grabs ALAN's hand). Thank you.
(REGINA's FATHER is suddenly emotional, TEE-TEE
gives him a tissue. Clearly she's been doing this a lot
lately.)

TEE-TEE. Here you go, Grandpa.

REGINA (to ALAN). The last couple of years have been
difficult for me, for us. (REGINA considers, then very

direct:) My husband passed away. Our son died of AIDS. I think losing them broke my heart. Really broke my heart, because it just gave out, it didn't want to beat anymore.

ALAN. I'm sorry.

REGINA. Being on the waiting list for a transplant... The waiting could kill you if the disease wasn't already planning that. I finally had to leave it up to God. One day I just said it: "God, I am in your hands." My family has been beautiful. My sister never left my side. My friends, my neighbors, my church, Pastor Quentin. The prayer circles. It's very humbling. I remember praying to God, saying "Lord, I hope I'm worth all this trouble."

PASTOR QUENTIN. "And all things—

PASTOR QUENTIN & REGINA'S MOTHER *(together)*. whatsoever ye shall ask in prayer—

ALL OF REGINA'S FAMILY & FRIENDS *(together)*. believing, ye shall receive." *(REGINA's MOTHER squeezes REGINA's hand.)*

TEE-TEE. It was my idea to have the party. Having Mama home—it's like New Year's.

ALAN *(remembering)*. L'Shana tova.

REGINA'S NEIGHBOR. What'd he call us?!?

ALAN *(laughing)*. It's something we say for the Jewish New Year. L'Shana tova—tikatevu. "Wishing you all sweet things for the New Year."

TEE-TEE *(trying to repeat the Hebrew)*. L'Shana—

ALAN. L'Shana tova—

TEE-TEE. L'Shana—tova—

ALAN. Tikatevu.

TEE-TEE. Tika—te—vu.

ALAN. L'Shana tova tikatevu.

TEE-TEE *(confident)*. L'Shana tova tikatevu.

ALAN. Excellent. You have an ear for Hebrew.

TEE-TEE. Well I'm part Jewish. *(Proud of herself.)* Happy New Year, Mama! May it be sweet sweet sweet!

REGINA *(to TEE-TEE)*. Thank you, Blessings. *(Beat.)* Is your father living, Alan?

ALAN. No, he died, years ago. It's just me and my sister now—but she had to get back to Chicago. Her job, her family… *(Really hitting him.)* It's just me. *(Beat.)* I've been going through my mother's things, you know…trying to put things in order. I had never read most of my mother's poetry— *(ALAN stops, he's on the edge emotionally.)*

REGINA. I'm so glad you decided to find me, that you came here—that I got to meet you.

ALAN. Really?

REGINA. I think God sent you.

ALAN. Or my mother.

REGINA. Well, sometimes the Lord works in mysterious ways.

ALAN. Ruth—may she rest in peace—would say it's b'shart, which means—

REGINA *(knowing the Hebrew)*. It was meant to be. *(ALAN nods. Beat.)* I feel a little more—peaceful. That's the word. Peaceful. Do you?

ALAN. Not really. But maybe I will. I think this all has to sink in. *(ALAN gets up to leave.)* Maybe I'll go to Temple. My mother always went to Temple, the older she got the more she went. I haven't been in a long time. Not sure what I'd—maybe just being there, you know? *(They walk to the front door.)* I can't thank you enough—

REGINA. Look who you're talking to! I'm the one who's thankful. *(She reaches out and takes ALAN's hands. They hold hands. ALAN suddenly realizes he feels REGINA's heartbeat in her hands.)*

ALAN. I feel—your heart. Beating.

(REGINA nods. Then she places ALAN's hand on her heart. ALAN feels the beating heart. For a long time. They don't look at each other. Then ALAN turns and leaves. REGINA stands at the open door looking out at the street. The porch light is on. The number "36" shines brightly against the house. REGINA looks up at the night sky. A huge full moon rises into view. TEE-TEE steps out and looks at REGINA.)

TEE-TEE. Mama? What are you doing?

REGINA *(still looking up at the sky)*. Looking at the moon, Blessings. Makes me feel closer to God somehow.

TEE-TEE. You feel OK?

REGINA. God existed before time, Jesus existed before pain. *(Reassuring TEE-TEE.)* I'm fine, baby. A little tired. But I'm fine. *(TEE-TEE puts her arms around REGINA, they both look up at the night sky.)* "The Lord is my shepherd; I shall not want. He maketh me to lie down in green pastures, he leadeth me beside the still waters. He restoreth my soul; he leadeth me in the paths of righteousness for his name's sake... Yea, though I walk through the valley of the shadow of death...

(The lights fade all around them. Slowly.)

SCENE FOUR: "Houston: We Have a Problem"
Black Aids: Black Faith / Buddhist

(Outer space. MUSIC. Otherworldly, weightless. The thick SOUND OF AMPLIFIED BREATHING. Lights up on black outer space speckled with stars and planets that glisten like jewels against black velvet. It's a beautiful setting full of mystery and impossibility. Like a slow-motion ballet: TWO ASTRONAUTS float into view, walking in space decked in full regalia. They are playfully giddy, turning slow motion somersaults, pirouetting, etc. Maybe they even play a game of one-on-one basketball in space. The tone should be playful and carefree. There is a sudden SOUND OF ALARMS, WARNING BELLS, PULSING BUZZING SOUND. The floating ASTRONAUTS instantly disappear and there is an aggressive bump up of lights to reveal: The interior of a U.S. spaceship—Beautiful Dreamer III. Lots of lighted buttons and switches. A curved glass window upstage of it all that opens up to pure black space. The TWO ASTRONAUTS sit at the controls. They wear spacesuits but no helmets. Both are men; one is black (REDWOOD), the other man is white (ANDERSON). REDWOOD is looking at an open Bible, reading to himself as he's listening to a voice from the control center:)

HOUSTON VOICE *(V.O.)*. Beautiful Dreamer—this is Houston. Here's what we know now. The main oxygen generator has failed and you may have to tap into the attached cargo ship air supply—

REDWOOD. There is no attached cargo ship—

HOUSTON VOICE. Damn it, Redwood, stay calm. There
   is no attached cargo ship YET. It arrives next week.
ANDERSON. Next week?
HOUSTON VOICE. And we have other back-up sources.
ANDERSON. Any idea what's causing the problem?
HOUSTON VOICE. It's the generator—
REDWOOD *(under his breath)*. Again.
ANDERSON *(to REDWOOD)*. Piece of Russian shit.
HOUSTON VOICE. I heard that, Anderson.
ANDERSON. Well it's not the first time that old Russian
   unit has tanked on us up here.
HOUSTON VOICE. Fair enough. But in the past the trou-
   ble has been air bubbles, this time it appears to be a
   blockage in a line.
REDWOOD *(frustrated)*. Great.
HOUSTON VOICE. We're confident we can get the gener-
   ator running again.
ANDERSON. And if you can't?
HOUSTON VOICE. We can. *(Beat.)* We will.
REDWOOD. But if you don't?
HOUSTON VOICE. If we don't… *(Beat.)* I won't lie to
   you, men. It's serious. Everyone down here is working
   around the clock to get the generator up and running
   again. Right now, the two of you need to sit tight.
ANDERSON *(glib)*. Where else we gonna go? *(To RED-
   WOOD.)* I hear Mars has got a Hooters on every
   crater… *(REDWOOD shakes his head, smiles in spite of
   himself.)*
HOUSTON VOICE. Sit tight and don't panic. *(The sound
   goes dead. The two ASTRONAUTS sit in silence staring
   straight ahead. Then:)*
ANDERSON. Shit. *(Beat.)*

REDWOOD. God help us.

ANDERSON *(ignores REDWOOD's comment).* It's cause and effect. The Program hasn't recovered since Columbia went down. Grounded the shuttle fleet, we're short of everything up here. Now we're even short of oxygen. What a pile of junk. *(Beat.)*

REDWOOD. Makes me miss my car.

ANDERSON. What do you drive?

REDWOOD. Beemer. Bronze Z3 Roadster. V6. Convertible. Heated seats. So sweet. *(Beat.)* You?

ANDERSON. '69 Impala. 427, four-on-the-floor. Green with a black hardtop. More mean than sweet. *(Beat. Both men lost in thoughts of home. The ALARMS start to sound again, PULSING SOUNDS, flashing lights. The two ASTRONAUTS flip switches, shout commands to each other:)* That's a master alarm!

REDWOOD. Multiple Caution & Warning. Number One Oxygen tank below 300 psi now.

ANDERSON. Still dropping?

REDWOOD. Dropping.

ANDERSON. Switching over to Omni-Bravo—

REDWOOD. Quad C to Quad A. *(And just as quickly everything returns to normal. But the effect is unnerving for both men. Now it's tense. REDWOOD pages through his small Bible, reads aloud:)* "The Lord is my shepherd; I shall not want. He maketh me to lie down in green pastures, he leadeth me beside the still waters. He restoreth my soul; he leadeth me in the paths of righteousness for his name's sake— *(Beat.)* "He restoreth my soul." He RESTORES me. *(REDWOOD looks over at ANDERSON.)* Pastor Andrew is right: you can read the same verses a hundred times...but then the 101st time it has a whole new meaning. *(REDWOOD closes his eyes, praying silently, then stops and looks at ANDERSON.)* Do you want to pray with me?

ANDERSON. Not really.

REDWOOD. It might help—

ANDERSON *(firm but not angry)*. I said no.

REDWOOD. You said "not really"—

ANDERSON. Well I meant "no." *(Beat.)*

REDWOOD. I mean, if there was ever a time to pray—this would be it. *(Beat.)* You do pray, right?

ANDERSON. Mmm. *(Beat.)*

REDWOOD. Is that a "yes mmm" or a "no mmm"?

ANDERSON. It's a "none of your business mmm."

REDWOOD *(hurt)*. Sorry. *(Beat.)*

ANDERSON. Look, Redwood—I don't pray, OK? I chant.

REDWOOD. What do you mean you chant?

ANDERSON. I'm a Buddhist. We chant.

REDWOOD. You're a Buddhist? *(Beat.)* I thought the Japanese were Buddhists.

ANDERSON. A lot of them are. *(Teasing.)* We're everywhere.

REDWOOD. Damn. I'm up here in space with a Buddhist.

ANDERSON. You don't hear me complaining about being up here with a Baptist.

REDWOOD. Methodist.

ANDERSON. Same thing.

REDWOOD *(indignant)*. Not if you're Methodist! *(Beat.)* But I still don't understand why you don't pray. Don't you have things you want to say to God?

ANDERSON. No.

REDWOOD. I bet he'd like to hear from you.

ANDERSON. I don't believe in God.

REDWOOD. Yes you do.

ANDERSON. No I don't.

REDWOOD. Are you saying that Buddhists don't believe in God?

ANDERSON. Correct. That's our dirty little secret.

REDWOOD. So you're really an atheist.

ANDERSON. No, I'm really a Buddhist.

REDWOOD. And you really don't believe in God?

ANDERSON. I really don't. Do you? Really?

REDWOOD. Of course I believe in God! How can you not believe in God?

ANDERSON. I don't think this is the time for a—

REDWOOD. Not the time?!? We are running out of oxygen, Anderson! We may be dead in a week. This is definitely the time. Wait a minute, you don't believe in God so you don't believe in heaven either? It doesn't matter to you if we live or die?

ANDERSON. Of course it matters. But no, I don't believe in heaven.

REDWOOD. Eternal life?

ANDERSON. Not eternal life. The ETERNITY of life.

REDWOOD. Come again?

ANDERSON. What do you believe will happen when you die?

REDWOOD. Well I hope I'll go to heaven.

ANDERSON. As yourself.

REDWOOD. Yeah. It's not a Halloween party where you get to show up as somebody else. Heaven is come as you are.

ANDERSON. Well we don't believe in a physical entity after death, there's no spirit or soul that continues to exist, no heaven.

REDWOOD. That's too bad. Especially considering the alternative. Wait, let me guess—you don't believe in hell either? How convenient.

ANDERSON. Hell is in the mind—heaven is in the heart.

REDWOOD. But what about that "eternity of life" business?

ANDERSON. You've heard of karma.

REDWOOD. Yeah. It's like the stuff you do.

ANDERSON. Right—action. So the "stuff you do" in THIS lifetime is the result of your actions in previous existences—

REDWOOD. Your karma—

ANDERSON. And our actions in the PRESENT determine the stuff in the future.

REDWOOD. "Do unto others as you would have them do unto you."

ANDERSON. Kinda.

REDWOOD. But what's all that got to do with the eternity of life?

ANDERSON. That's what I'm trying to tell you. It's not the INDIVIDUAL that goes on after death, it's the ACTIONS of the individual. The ACTIONS, the KARMA is what goes on after death. The eternity of life. *(Long silence. REDWOOD returns to silently reading his Bible. Then:)*

REDWOOD. But don't you think it's bad karma not to believe in God?

ANDERSON *(laughing)*. That's a very Christian thing to say.

REDWOOD. Well I AM a Christian. *(Beat.)* And I'd feel a lot better if you'd say a prayer or something. *(Beat.)*

ANDERSON. I could chant.

REDWOOD. Out loud?

ANDERSON. I've been dying to hear what it sounds like in space. Doing it in my head all these months—it's not the same thing. *(REDWOOD seems to be thinking it over.)* At home I chant every day. When I don't—I'm a tired, irritable, mean, nasty, did I say irritable? self-righteous, negative, judgmental, weak person who is ALWAYS RIGHT.

REDWOOD. Dude, you should have been chanting a long time ago then.

ANDERSON *(laughing)*. I'll chant—you can pray. We'll do it at the same time. *(Joking:)* Hey, it doubles our chance of survival, one of us is bound to be right. *(Beat.)*

REDWOOD. I can't believe I'm up here with a Buddhist. I don't think I've ever even known a Buddhist, I think you're the first one. And just because you're going to chant doesn't mean you can try and convert me or something.

ANDERSON *(laughing)*. Deal. *(Beat.)* Who goes first?

REDWOOD. We'll go at the same time. Countdown from three.

REDWOOD & ANDERSON *(together)*. Three…two…one—

(They freeze, hauntingly remain on stage and we are instantly in the next scene:)

SCENE FIVE: "Location, Location, Location"
Buddhist / Atheist

(Santa Monica. An empty house with a "For Sale" sign in front. Daytime. An Asian woman [DIANA] leads a family out of the house. It's a husband [AJAY] and wife [LISA] and THREE KIDS ages 6-16. And a DOG. The grownups stand by the "For Sale" sign; the three kids do their own things in the yard. The YOUNGEST and MIDDLE KID roughhouse, tumbling, shouting; the TEENAGER stands off to the side talking on a cell phone.)

DIANA. ...so what do you think? I mean compared to everything we've seen—does it give you the feeling? Is this the one?

YOUNGEST KID. I like the pool!

MIDDLE KID. Are we gonna buy it, Dad?

YOUNGEST KID. I like the pool! *(The TWO YOUNGER KIDS run into the yard and wrestle each other to the ground.)*

AJAY *(to LISA)*. I like that it's solar.

LISA *(nodding)*. And the backyard is to die for. I didn't expect to find a place with so much space.

AJAY *(agreeing)*. The kitchen is amazing.

LISA. The kids will finally each have their own rooms.

DIANA. It's a great place. I think you'd be happy here. *(AJAY and LISA look at each other, they're excited but torn, not fully committing.)*

AJAY. Maybe we should think it over—

LISA *(agreeing)*. If it's still here in a week, it was meant to be.

DIANA *(inserting herself)*. I thought you were in a hurry to buy. The market in Santa Monica is still hot, this place won't last. *(LISA and AJAY look at each other.)*

LISA. I don't know.

AJAY. It's more than we wanted to pay.

DIANA. But it has everything you're looking for, everything you said you wanted.

AJAY. Looked like a lot of termite damage in the garage—

DIANA. We can negotiate for the seller to pay for that.

LISA. Property taxes are going to be steep.

AJAY. The house is awfully white—

DIANA. You'll paint it. That's the fun part. *(AJAY and LISA look at each other, DIANA senses she's losing ground on the sale. More aggressive.)* This house has a beautiful vibe—did you feel it? *(AJAY and LISA look at DIANA.)* ...there's something so—spiritual—about it. *(AJAY and LISA look at each other, uncomfortable now. DIANA continues, going for broke:)* Lisa. Ajay. Listen to me: if there's something I know about—it's houses. Every day I'm looking at houses and most of them lack something. Sometimes people don't know how to describe it—but I can tell by the way they're uncomfortable that it's the house VIBE that turns them off. It's the lack of spirituality—in the house. One woman told me that if she walks into a house and doesn't want to pray then she knows it's not the house for her. Why don't you go back in the house without me. Just go in, close your eyes, see if you get the feeling. See if you don't agree with me—see if you don't feel something spiritual about this house.

AJAY. Um—

DIANA. Yes?

AJAY. Well— *(He looks at LISA.)*

LISA. Diana—

DIANA. Yes? *(Tense pause.)*

LISA. We're really grateful for the time you've taken with us.

DIANA. That's my job.

LISA. We appreciate it.

DIANA. Thank you.

LISA. But we have to be honest with you—

AJAY. We really hate that word.

DIANA. Which word?

AJAY. "Spiritual." Hate it.

DIANA *(surprised)*. Oh.

LISA. It's just that it sounds—supernatural or something.

DIANA. Oh I didn't mean it in the negative way, I didn't mean that the house is haunted. It's more that it's—special. It's special in a spiritual way.

AJAY *(grimacing)*. Yeah, that word—spiritual—it's just a big, big turn-off.

DIANA. Oh. *(To LISA.)* For you too? *(LISA nods.)* Wow.

LISA. It's just that, we're not—

LISA & AJAY *(simultaneous)*. religious.

DIANA *(getting it)*. Oh God! Sorry. So many people I show houses to talk about "the vibe"—you'd be surprised how many people bring up God or religion when they're buying a house. I guess I made an assumption.

AJAY. Yeah.

LISA. We're not looking for a house that's spiritual or religious. That's really not important to us.

AJAY. Actually we could care less about all that.

DIANA. Wow.

LISA. I'm sorry if that makes you uncomfortable—

DIANA. No, no—

(Simultaneous:)

AJAY.	LISA.
We don't believe in—	We're not part of all that—

DIANA. Right.

AJAY. We're atheists. Well I am. Lisa calls herself a humanist.

LISA. People hear the word "atheist" and they immediately get negative. Not that you were being negative. I mean, we really like you, and we don't want to offend you—

AJAY. Leela, why are you apologizing?

DIANA. Leela? I thought your name was Lisa.

LISA. It's both. I mean, Lisa is just easier to spell.

AJAY. Maybe we should work with another realtor. The whole religious thing just puts a spin on this, you know.

LISA. It comes down to trust. Who can you trust?

DIANA. I owe you an apology.

LISA. No, really, that's not necessary.

AJAY. Yes it is.

LISA. Ajay—

AJAY *(to LISA, testy)*. Well, I don't appreciate the assumption that we're religious. I'm so tired of having to articulate and contextualize everything through this Judeo-Christian lens. What a bunch of smoke and mirrors. My kids say the Pledge of Allegiance and want to know what's under God. They look at the dollar bill and it says "In God We Trust"—and they want to know why WE don't trust in God. Our youngest was an angel in the Christmas program at school. Don't get me started. I mean, everything about our neighborhood is so—you want to know why we're moving? One of our neighbors told our twelve-year-old that if his parents didn't believe in God then maybe we should leave the country. In America, being an atheist is the same as being a devil-worshipper—which is funny because, of course, I don't believe in the devil either.

YOUNGEST KID. I want to be a devil for Halloween!

AJAY. You are a devil!

LISA. I'm sorry, Diana. He gets like this when he doesn't eat lunch.

AJAY. Stop apologizing for me. *(AJAY goes to his YOUNG SON, the MIDDLE KID joins in and the three of them play. LISA and DIANA watch.)*

LISA. We run into this all the time—we just didn't think we'd have to deal with it today, I mean with you, I mean with real estate. We just want to buy a house, you know? We just want to find a home.

DIANA. I really do owe you an apology. I'm sorry.

LISA. Thank you. *(DIANA looks up at the sky.)* Diana? *(DIANA doesn't answer, continues to look up at the sky. Then she begins to laugh. First in fits and starts, then uncontrollably. AJAY and YOUNG KID look over. The laughter continues. It goes on for a little too long. AJAY and the TWO YOUNGER KIDS join LISA who continues staring at DIANA.)* Are you OK?

DIANA *(still laughing)*. It's so absurd! *(She's reduced to wild laughter again.)* I'm a Buddhist.

MIDDLE KID. What did she say?

DIANA *(gaining composure)*. I'm a Buddhist. *(LISA and AJAY are a little surprised, but visibly relax.)*

LISA. Well that's a relief.

DIANA. Is it?

LISA. Sure. I assumed you were—something else. Something—MORE. I don't mean that the wrong way. I'm sure Buddhists are a lot—I mean FULL, full of Buddhism. That didn't come out right.

DIANA *(laughing)*. It's all right! I have no idea what you're talking about.

AJAY. You're pretty pushy for a Buddhist. I had a roommate in college who was a Nichiren Buddhist, he was really mellow.

DIANA. Oh, that's not me. They chant, I don't chant. My husband chants. Yes, yes—it's a mixed marriage. A Nichiren Buddhist and a Zen Buddhist... We're like the James Carville and Mary Matlin of Buddhism. My husband's a convert—they're so strict, you know, converts. Major pains in the ass.

AJAY. Buddhists are atheists, right?

DIANA. I think that's our dirty little secret—at least in America. We don't believe in a God—I mean, Buddha isn't God. I don't even think of Buddhism as a religion. It's my life, you know, it's how I grew up. Sometimes it's hard to know what's Buddhism, what's Chinese, what's my family, what's culture. It's all tangled up.

AJAY. But people don't hassle you about Buddhism—

DIANA. True. Sometimes they even seem a little starry-eyed when they find out I'm a Buddhist.

AJAY. Well we don't get that reaction. Starry-eyed isn't how people respond. When I declared myself an atheist—I was in college. I remember going home for Christmas break, and my parents begged me to call myself agnostic—they didn't care what I believed, they cared more about what other people would THINK about what I believed. You have to take a stand, you know? I don't believe in God. In Kingdom Come. In re-incarnation. I believe in other things. The Here and Now. My family, my work. I even believe in our country—proof that an atheist can be an optimist. *(Beat.)* At some point, it becomes clear that you have to choose the things you're going to go deep with in your life. *(DIANA and LISA nod. The three of them are silent, lost in thought. LISA looks over at their son who's still talking on the cell phone.)*

LISA. Our oldest believes in God. That's the crazy thing.

DIANA. Really?

AJAY *(shrugs)*. We got soft on Santa Claus—turned out to be good practice for believing in other things that don't exist. *(AJAY, LISA and DIANA laugh.)*

LISA. The other day our youngest asked me if "God" is a nickname for "Godfrey."

DIANA. Three kids and a dog... You wouldn't believe how envious I am of that.

LISA. What do you mean?

DIANA. Well, you can pass. If you need to, I mean. If you're the perfect all-American family who's going to question whether or not you believe in God.

AJAY. WE'RE the perfect all-American family???

DIANA. Compared to me and my husband? You can look the part and get away with it.

AJAY. We don't do that.

DIANA. Never?

AJAY. Never. *(Beat.)*

LISA. Do you have kids?

DIANA. Not yet. But we're planning on it. Someday. *(Beat.)* My husband has been away for months.

AJAY. Military?

DIANA. NASA.

LISA. He's an astronaut? Wow.

YOUNGEST KID. Who's an astronaut?

AJAY. Diana's husband is an astronaut.

YOUNGEST KID. Cool! Three-two-one-BLASTOFF!!!
(The YOUNG KID pretends to be flying through outer space—SOUND EFFECTS and all. DIANA looks up at the sky. LISA looks up at the sky and then suddenly back at DIANA.)

LISA *(concerned)*. Is he—

DIANA. Yeah.

AJAY. Your husband is one of the guys, in the—? Are they OK?

DIANA *(covering)*. They're fine.

LISA. But what are you doing here? Why are you working?

DIANA. They're fine. *(LISA and AJAY look at each other.)* They're telling us that they're fine. Everything's gonna be—fine. *(Beat.)* It's just the waiting, you know. I'd rather stay busy. *(Beat.)*

AJAY. Do they know—about your husband? I mean, that he's a Buddhist?

DIANA. NASA? No. They have a kind of a "don't ask, don't tell" policy about religion. *(Beat.)*

LISA. I can't believe your husband is one of those astronauts.

DIANA *(looking up)*. I miss him. *(Beat.)* I go to sleep at night with my bedroom window open so I can see the sky. I close my eyes and sometimes I swear I can hear him chanting.

(Onstage [in space], ANDERSON begins to chant:)

ANDERSON *(repeating over and over).* "Nam-myoho-renge-kyo"

(REDWOOD watches ANDERSON chant. ANDERSON continues to chant while motioning for REDWOOD to join in as promised. REDWOOD finally closes his eyes and begins to say the Lord's Prayer:)

REDWOOD. "Our Father, who art in heaven, hallowed be thy name…" *(The ASTRONAUTS continue chanting and praying under the real estate scene:)*

LISA. I like this house. *(Beat.)* I can see us living here. *(Beat.)* It has everything we want.

DIANA. But what if I'm right? *(Uncomfortable.)* What if it IS—the house, you know—spiritual?

AJAY. It's not. *(The TWO YOUNGER KIDS run after the dog. The TEENAGER continues to talk on the cell phone.)*

REDWOOD.	ANDERSON.
Thy Kingdom come, thy will be done, on earth as it is in heaven. Give us this day our daily bread. Forgive us our trespasses as we forgive those who trespass against us. And lead us not into temptation, but deliver us from evil. For thine is the kingdom, and the power, and the glory forever.	Nam-myoho-renge-kyo, Nam-myoho-renge-kyo, Nam-myoho-renge-kyo, Nam-myoho-renge-kyo, Nam-myoho-renge-kyo, Nam-myoho-renge-kyo, Nam-myoho-renge-kyo, Nam-myoho-renge-kyo, Nam-myoho-renge-kyo, Nam-myoho-renge-kyo, Nam-myoho-renge-kyo, Nam-myoho-renge-kyo, Nam-myoho-renge-kyo, Nam-myoho-renge-kyo…

(They continue to pray and chant and we suddenly hear ALARMS/WARNING BELLS/HOUSTON/STATIC. <SOUND OF ALARMS/WARNING BELLS/HOUSTON> the praying, chanting and alarms continue simultaneously. And then like a plug has been pulled, everything is silent. Then the lights go black.)

INTERMISSION

ACT TWO

*When we return from intermission, the actors who per-
formed in the contemporary scenes from Act One are no
longer on stage. The remaining actors are still dressed
in their Biblical garb, sitting in the chairs. MRS.
STEVENSON addresses us again, this time she is a little
more introspective, unsure what will happen next.*

MRS. STEVENSON. Hello again, welcome back. I'm told
we're almost ready to begin Act Two. I must tell
you—this is quite different from the play that I wrote. I
overheard one of you talking in the powder room during
intermission about a recent controversy over the image
of a cross in the Los Angeles county seal. I'm sure
many of you have seen that big cross on the hill, right
over there. *(Humble.)* You probably don't know that that
cross is a memorial to me. After my death in 1922, some
dear Hollywood friends erected a forty-foot cross in my
memory. It had 1800 incandescent light bulbs in it. For
years the Southern California Edison Company paid the
electric bill—can you imagine? When a fire damaged
the cross in 1965, the county replaced it with that new
cross. It's lit every night. *(MRS. STEVENSON gestures
to the many PILGRIMAGE PLAYERS still on stage, still
in Biblical garb.)* For those of us who haunt this place—

that cross is our night light. *(Beat.)* 1964 was the last time my play was performed here. A lawsuit forced its closure due to its religious nature. *(Quietly.)* Let us begin Act Two. *(MRS. STEVENSON takes her place off to the side, eager to see what happens in Act Two.*

SCENE SIX: "There Must Be Some Mistake"
Atheist / Baha'i

(Pasadena. The living room of an Iranian-American family. A MOTHER and FATHER, their DAUGHTER and their SISTER-IN-LAW have all gathered in the family living room. The daughter [OMEED] is 15 years old and dressed like a "typical 21st-century California teenager." She is holding a small bundle of letters. AJAY [the husband from the previous scene] sits with the family. He has a notepad. A tape recorder is set up on a table. There is a long silence. No one moves, no one breathes. We are not at the beginning of the scene—we have come in the middle of a difficult moment. Everyone is trying to regain composure. The MOTHER gets up and picks up a framed photograph, hands it to AJAY to look at. Finally AJAY tries to start again:)

AJAY. I know this is difficult—
FATHER. You know? How do you know?
AJAY. You're right. I don't know. But I can imagine. I'm a father, too.

FATHER. You can't imagine! No one can imagine. To lose your child, in a war, in THIS war? The irony—it chokes me.

AJAY. The irony? *(Beat.)* Being Muslim, you mean? *(All of the FAMILY MEMBERS look at one another, at AJAY, shocked.)*

MOTHER. Muslim?

FATHER. We are not Muslim.

AJAY *(shuffling through his notes)*. I'm sorry, I was told that you were Muslim.

FATHER. Because we came here from Iran?

MOTHER. We are not Muslim—

SISTER-IN-LAW. We are members of the Baha'i faith.

AJAY *(nodding)*. Baha'i. I apologize. The paper, I was told—

MOTHER. We are Baha'is.

AJAY. Yes. Baha'i. Sorry. *(Beat.)* When did you leave? When did you come to Los Angeles?

MOTHER. 1983.

FATHER. The fundamentalists were coming down hard on the Baha'is in Iran, my brother was killed. My wife's brother was killed too.

SISTER-IN-LAW. My husband.

AJAY. Why?

SISTER-IN-LAW. You really don't know?

AJAY. I'm a journalist—I can't quote myself.

FATHER. Because they were Baha'is! They were killed because they were Baha'is in a Muslim country—

SISTER-IN-LAW. A FUNDAMENTALIST Muslim country.

FATHER. A fundamentalist Muslim country. To be a Baha'i, to be the minority— *(The FATHER pauses, looks at AJAY, then dismisses him.)* You wouldn't understand.

AJAY. Help me understand. You left Iran because—

FATHER *(irritated)*. Because I was next! Because I was in hiding. Because it was clear that I would be killed if we stayed. *(Awkward beat.)*

MOTHER. Do you know that in Tehran—Roosevelt Street and Kennedy Square have been replaced with the names of terrorists?

SISTER-IN-LAW. That is the country we left behind. It was our home.

MOTHER. Now—it's just a ghost inside me.

AJAY. Do any of you feel—sometimes—that America is a fundamentalist country? *(The question hangs in the air, goes unanswered. Then:)*

MOTHER. We came to America, we came for freedom. And now my son has died fighting for freedom. Operation Iraqi Freedom. That's what we were told.

AJAY. Do you believe that, that he was fighting for freedom?

FATHER. Does it matter what we believe? Our son is dead. He has died in a war—in a country next door to the country he was born in. He was killed trying to liberate the people, killed trying to liberate the Iraqi Muslim people! The same people who wanted him and his family dead in Iran. That is the irony. Sons of sons of sons... Did I save myself only to kill my son— *(The FATHER breaks down, crying. The MOTHER comforts him.)*

MOTHER *(to her husband)*. No, it isn't like that. You cannot believe that.

AJAY *(to the MOTHER)*. Are you able to talk about your son? What was he like?

MOTHER. A mother talks about her children because she knows them even with her eyes closed. The way they smell. Their small hands. Their voices. Every day they leave their fingerprints on you. *(Beat.)* Baha'u'llah says, "I have made Death a messenger of joy. Wherefore dost thou grieve?" Are you a religious man, Mr. Shah?

AJAY *(careful)*. No. To be honest, I'm— *(beat)* not.

MOTHER. Does my suffering make you feel superior then?

AJAY. Excuse me?

MOTHER *(genuine)*. I wonder if suffering is more bearable if you don't believe in God. At least you don't have to wonder why. Why would God let such a thing happen? *(Beat.)*

AJAY. Would it be all right if I ask your daughter a few questions?

MOTHER *(looks at OMEED)*. That would be up to her. *(Tense.)* She refuses to talk to us anyway.

(AJAY turns his attention to OMEED—she looks at him, still clutching the packet of letters. She shrugs, looks away.)

AJAY. Are those letters from your brother?

MOTHER. She won't let us read them.

(OMEED looks at her MOTHER, then holds out a letter for AJAY to read. He can't resist. As AJAY opens the letter, a huge projected image of a soldier [SHAHAB] appears on a wall in the room. He speaks directly to us:)

SHAHAB *(on video)*. Hey, little sister…it's ShahAb. Happy Birthday! How are you? How's school? What can I tell you? Not much to report… It was 130 degrees today. The days are just hot and dusty, at night it's chilly. Can you ask Mom to send me one of my old hoodies? Send me one that has UCLA on it. Go Bruins! *(Beat.)* I got into a little accident—I'm fine. We were hit by an IED, set our truck on fire. I lost my hearing in my left ear for a few weeks. I got most of it back. Don't tell Mom and Dad, OK? *(Beat.)* They're saying there's no way we're going home in less than twelve months. I don't know how we'll make it—it already seems like I've been here twice as long as I have. *(Beat.)* My life seems far away. In some ways, I don't think I'll ever have it back again. I think war takes certain things from you, or maybe it gives certain things that changes your perspective—I guess I don't know yet. *(Beat.)* It's night. The stars are amazing. I've never seen skies so black, stars so bright. It really does feel biblical here. In Genesis it says that God made four rivers—and two of them are right here in Iraq…the Tigris and the Euphrates. I had to go down and touch the water, you know? I waded in and looked back to where Baha'u'llah revealed the Hidden Words as he walked along the banks of the Tigris. I just stood in the water. I just stood in the Tigris River—and felt myself drawing nearer to God…

AJAY *(looks up from the letter. To OMEED)*. How—as a Baha'i—how do you reconcile—

OMEED *(grabs the letter from AJAY and exits the room angrily)* I am not a Baha'i!

(The video image of SHAHAB suddenly disconnects and disappears. Silence.)

MOTHER. Omeed was born in this country—her brother ShahAb was born in Iran. I think this is all very different for her.

AJAY. Do you believe in this war? That it's right?

MOTHER. Since the end of Sadaam's regime, Iraqi Baha'is are free to practice their religion for the first time in more than thirty years.

AJAY. Then you DO believe that this war—

SISTER-IN-LAW. Baha'is believe that the Earth is but one country, and mankind its citizens. We work and pray that all conflicts will be resolved—and peacefully if possible...

AJAY *(pointing out the irony)*. Peacefully.

MOTHER. If possible.

FATHER *(the last word)*. It is not the practice of the Baha'i faith to take positions on the political decisions of the government. *(Beat.)*

MOTHER. There is a house in Baghdad—a house where Baha'u'llah lived while in exile. For Baha'is—Iraq is a place of pilgrimage.

AJAY. So maybe your son made that pilgrimage in his own way. *(Beat.)*

MOTHER. Do you know, Mr. Shah, that the United States government provides gravemarkers for the military? They give you choices...they show you pictures, emblems to choose from—there is your Christian cross, and the Hebrew Star of David, the Muslim Crescent and Star, one for the Buddhists and the Hindu, and the Mormons and the Christian Scientists. The Unitarians have a gravestone too. Even the atheists have their own special gravestone. *(AJAY looks up from his notes—obviously this is something he didn't know.)* And the Baha'is. Our own military gravestone from the U.S. government. It's the 9-Pointed Star. It's a small thing—but it's huge too. My son lived and died a Baha'i. We don't have to hide that—even in his death. It's the one thing, for now, that I am grateful for. We are not in hiding, Mr. Shah. We're in mourning.

(AJAY nods. They sit in more silence. A projection of a photo appears on a wall. It is a picture of the son (SHAHAB) in American military uniform. The photo grows larger and larger and larger—haunting and over-whelming the room. And the lights slowly fade. In the dark, in the transition to the next scene, the MOTHER pulls up a chair and sits facing a wall where more projected images begin to flicker, and slowly transition into grainy home movies...a little boy with his little sister, horsing around, running, at the beach, making faces at the camera, carefree, alive...)

SCENE SEVEN: "Declaration"
Baha'i / Hindu

(Hollywood. A theater/dance performance. Community production in Hindu Temple. Sitting in an audience watching the performance is OMEED [the 15 year-old daughter] from the previous scene. She watches, rapt. Sitting next to her is her brother SHAHAB [the dead soldier] from the previous scene. He is dressed in contem-

*porary street clothes, longer hair than the previous
scene. We have gone back in time, six months before his
death. The performance is based on the Hindu story of
Lord Vishnu assuming the form of the beautiful female
dancer named Mohini as a way of intervening on behalf
of Lord Shiva—to destroy the king of demons, Bhasmasura.
The production is athletic and fast-paced. There are
dancers and puppets, music. A STAGEHAND is visible
to us—he is making all the sound effects and is a show
in and of himself. The tone is free-wheeling, irreverent,
funny. While true to the traditional Mohini-Attam dance
form, it is also freely reinvented by the performers.)*

STORYTELLER. Ladies and gentleman! Welcome to the
    Malibu Temple—and our performance of the story of
    Mohini. *(Beat.)* In the beginning of our story, the Great
    God Shiva—also known as the "Simpleton God" by his
    frustrated followers—is about to grant a demon—

BHASMASURA. A TERRIBLE demon!

STORYTELLER. As I was saying, the Great God Shiva is
    about to grant a TERRIBLE demon the ability to turn
    anything the demon touches into ASH. Lord Shiva is do-
    ing this out of fear, because he desperately wants to
    please the demon.

LORD SHIVA. "I, Lord Shiva, do bestow this gift upon you:
        Anyone you should touch on the head with your
        hand—
        Will themselves turn to ASH!
        Ash at your command."

BHASMASURA *(pleased with himself)*. I am Bhasmasura,
    the Ash-Demon, I am! *(Suddenly troubled.)*

But how do I know you are true to your word?

How do I know you don't mock me like a bird?

LORD SHIVA. Please, I beg you! Don't be absurd.

BHASMASURA. No! I must test my new world-conquering boon!

LORD SHIVA. His words that pour forth are blah-blah and jejune.

BHASMASURA. Whose head will I touch first?

Let me see, let me see…

Whose head will I touch first?

Could it be, could it be…

I choose, I choose, I choose

(Pointing to LORD SHIVA.) HE!

LORD SHIVA *(stunned)*. You can't choose me!

BHASMASURA. Lord Shiva himself, I choose THEE!

(BHASMASURA reaches out to touch SHIVA's head and SHIVA escapes the touch at the last possible moment.)

LORD SHIVA *(incredulous)*.

But one cannot slay the same one who crowned you,

It isn't polite, it isn't—Hindu!

BHASMASURA *(seductive)*. Just one touch, Lord Shiva, as gentle as the breeze!

I promise my touch to be as surprising as a sneeze.

Just one touch, Lord Shiva, soft as an eyelash…

One touch to your head, and you'll turn into ASH!

LORD SHIVA. Excuse me, forgive me, but now I must DASH! *(He makes a run for it, BHASMASURA chasing after him.)*

STORYTELLER. Lord Shiva is chased by the Ash-Demon through every corner of the universe.

(Dance of BHASMASURA chasing SHIVA.)

STORYTELLER *(cont'd)*. Finally, Lord Shiva finds a hiding place where he's convinced he is safe.

LORD SHIVA *(out of breath)*. I've lost him, I've lost him,
I thought I was dead—

BHASMASURA *(calling out, sweetly)*.

Lord Shiva? Lord Shiva?

Please let me touch your lord-ly head!

LORD SHIVA. There is only one who can save me from
turning to dust,

I must find Lord Vishnu! Only he can I trust.

STORYTELLER. And so the terrified Lord Shiva sets out
to find Vishnu—the trickster god who can usually be
found sleeping.

(Dance of LORD SHIVA finding the sleeping VISHNU.)

LORD SHIVA. Vishnu, old friend!

You MUST save my life!

Awake now, awake now, awake now, awake!

VISHNU. I'm awake, I'm awake, NOW what am I saving
you from???

LORD SHIVA. A monster, a snake, a demon on the make!

I admit it, I did it, I granted his wish—

VISHNU. That was childish! That was foolish!

That was truly, truly stupid…ish!

LORD SHIVA. I know, don't say it, it's already been
said—

BHASMASURA *(calling out sweetly)*.

Lord Shiva? Lord Shiva!

Please let me touch your lord-ly head!

VISHNU. But what were you thinking? And why, when
and how?

LORD SHIVA *(annoyed, panicked)*. Vishnu, no questions, just do something NOW!

VISHNU. I'm thinking—

BHASMASURA. Lord Shiva???

LORD SHIVA *(to VISHNU, urgent)*. Think faster!

(Dance of VISHNU assuming the form of the enchantress MOHINI, a beautiful female dancer. LORD SHIVA watches the transformation, amazed.)

LORD SHIVA *(cont'd)*. Wow.

STORYTELLER. At that moment, Vishnu transformed himself into the beautiful Mohini—a male god in female flesh.

(LORD SHIVA hides but we can see him watching what happens: BHASMASURA runs on, and stops when he sees the beautiful MOHINI/VISHNU who is dancing her alluring dance. It is like casting a magic spell.)

STORYTELLER *(cont'd)*. For Bhasmasura—it was love at first sight.

BHASMASURA. Oh beauty! Most beauty, we'll marry by sunset! *(BHASMASURA reaches out to touch MOHINI and he/she barely escapes his touch—continuing to dance.)*

MOHINI/VISHNU. You must not touch me—

You must not touch me yet.

One is but solo, and two a duet.

(Mesmerized, BHASMASURA begins to mimic MOHINI's every move. MOHINI/VISHNU continue:)

Move as I move, dance as I dance…

BHASMASURA. Move as you move…dance as you dance… *(BHASMASURA keeps up with MOHINI surprisingly well, gesturing and posturing.)*

MOHINI/VISHNU. Move as I move, dance as I dance…

BHASMASURA. Move as you move…dance as you dance…

MOHINI/VISHNU. Do as I say…

BHASMASURA. Do as you said…

MOHINI/VISHNU. Hands to your heart…

(Then MOHINI suddenly puts her hand on her head and BHASMASURA—distracted by her beauty and grace—does the same thing.)

BHASMASURA. Hands to my head.

(Suddenly BHASMASURA is burned by his own touch, and is reduced to ashes, dying on the spot. LORD SHIVA jumps out of hiding.)

LORD SHIVA. Vishnu! You saved me—you saved all the world!

MOHINI/VISHNU. Sometimes true power, is inside the girl.

(Celebration dance.)

STORYTELLER. The end.

(As the performance ends, the on-stage audience applauds and the actors take their bows. Then OMEED

*and SHAHAB get up and begin talking about the perfor-
mance:)*

SHAHAB. So what did you think?

OMEED. I liked it. I liked the costumes.

SHAHAB. Yes, and...??? What about the story? What did
you think about the story?

OMEED. I liked the part—where that guy, becomes that
woman—

SHAHAB. Vishnu becomes Mohini.

OMEED. Right. I liked the way she danced.

SHAHAB. If only every man had a smart woman living inside him, someone who could save the world.

OMEED. So now we can cross Hindus off the list.

SHAHAB. What list?

OMEED. Your list, "ShahAb's List." All these religions
you keep forcing on me.

SHAHAB. You said you liked this one—

OMEED.	SHAHAB.
I did, but as much as I liked it, ShahAb—I know that I'm not a Hindu. And I'm not a	
Jew. And I'm not a Muslim.	How do you know?
And I'm not a Christian.	How do you know?
And I'm not a Buddhist—	How do you know?
and I'm not—	How do you know?

OMEED *(impatient)*. I know!

SHAHAB *(stronger)*. How?!? How do you know???

OMEED. Because I'm a Baha'i!

SHAHAB. Not until you learn about all other religions—

OMEED. But I was BORN a Baha'i—

SHAHAB *(insistent)*. No one is born a Baha'i, Omeed. It isn't a birthright, it isn't something that's handed to you, you have to search.

OMEED *(frustrated)*. Why couldn't I just have a normal brother?

SHAHAB *(laughing)*. Who wants to be normal? Look: I believe you are an amazing person, little sister.

OMEED. But you act like you don't want me to be a Baha'i. Why do you have to push me?

SHAHAB. I'm not pushing. Think of it more like turning on the lights. Study, think, investigate. If you simply declare yourself a Baha'i because you were born into it, then you're missing one of the beautiful parts of our faith. Learn about other religions! They all have something to say to us, all the prophets bring us closer to God. *(Beat.)*

OMEED. You know what's weird? If I were born into any other religion, they would be so happy to have me—because I really want to be IN IT, you know? My friends in school don't care about religion, about ANY religion. And here I am, ready to throw myself into my faith, ready to give myself completely, to love God and study Baha'i for the rest of my life—and you don't want me to.

SHAHAB. Omeed—

OMEED. It's so messed up.

SHAHAB. Of course I want you to. I have no doubt that on your fifteenth birthday you will declare yourself a Baha'i—but it's the CHOICE, it's having the CHOICE to declare yourself a Baha'i that makes it so incredible. If you don't give yourself that choice, then you lose the chance to go deeper with yourself, to go deeper with God. *(Beat. OMEED nods. Beat.)*

OMEED. Have you told Mom and Dad that you joined the Marines?

SHAHAB. Not yet.

OMEED. Mmm.

(OMEED walks off, SHAHAB watches her go, then follows after her as the lights fade.)

SCENE EIGHT: "Spanish 101 for Two Hindus and a Muslim"
Hindu / Muslim

(Westwood. A UCLA dorm room. Colorfully decorated— one side of the room with Hindu stuff, the other side of the room with Muslim stuff. Both sides have lots of American pop culture too. It's a funny smorgasbord. A laptop and textbook are both open on one of the beds. On a rug rolled out next to that bed, SHAMA is doing her daily prayers [in Arabic]. She's a 19 year-old Muslim woman, wears the Hijab scarf.)

SHAMA. <PRAYERS>

(JAYANTI and SANGITA burst into the room laughing hysterically at something one has just said before entering. They're carrying coffee cups from Starbucks. Both are 19-20 years old, both Hindu—Indian. [JAYANTI is the same woman who played VISHNU/MOHINI in the dance theater piece in the previous scene.] They get

quiet when they see SHAMA praying, JAYANTI entering and plopping on her side of the room. SANGITA hangs back, uncomfortable about entering, JAYANTI motions to her to come in. SHAMA continues her prayers. JAYANTI opens a textbook; SANGITA can't help but look over at SHAMA who continues praying. They talk quietly under SHAMA's prayers:)

SANGITA. Does it feel weird, that she does that in your room?

JAYANTI. At first it did. But now I think, "Wow. We never do that. We're just not that dedicated."

SANGITA. I used to watch my grandma do her personal worship in the mornings. She'd carefully wash her hands and then pray to her baby Krishna. If I told her I didn't say my prayers because I didn't have a Krishna, she'd say, "You can find God anywhere. In India you can pick up a rock, say it's God, and people will pray to it. It's all fine." I loved her. *(Glancing over at SHAMA.)* She taught me that when you offer flowers to God, you don't smell them first. That's for God. *(Looking at SHAMA again.)* She talked to God too—she said he made her laugh.

JAYANTI. When my grandma came here to visit the first time, we thought she'd love Artesia, you know, all the Indian fabrics. But you know what she loved? Ikea. My grandma from Ludhiana loved Ikea. She kept wanting to go back, kept saying that Ikea was very Hindu. We were like, "What are you talking about?" And she said, "Ikea—it's very Hindu! They're both big, they're both colorful. And you think about going to Ikea because there's always something there for you, even if you're not sure what it is before you get there… You always find something that you need at Ikea—just like being Hindu." *(SANGITA is watching SHAMA.)* I talk to God.

SANGITA. Really?

JAYANTI *(nodding)*. Yeah. I talk to God in my car. Driving—I have the most interesting arguments with God. Last week I was driving to the Vedanta Center, it was pouring rain—I could hardly see where I was going. I was having a fight with God about a fight I'd had with my mother—and suddenly the rain just…stopped. And there was this amazing rainbow in the sky—in L.A. It was a Darshan, a vision— I pulled my car over and just looked at it. I didn't know if God was saying he had won the argument, or if he was trying to distract me. Or if he just wanted me to connect—to myself. Because there was something about that rainbow…it hit me, really hit me—"I Am He"—you know? I am God. *(Beat.)* Still—I'm going to keep it a secret from my grandparents that I eat meat sometimes. *(They laugh, SANGITA distracted by SHAMA's praying.)*

SANGITA. I thought you said she didn't wear the scarf in your room.

JAYANTI. She doesn't. Sometimes she does. She wears it when she prays. I don't know.

SANGITA. You ever ask her about it?

JAYANTI. About the scarf?

SANGITA. Yeah. Why does she wear it?

JAYANTI. She's Muslim.

SANGITA. So. Lots of Muslim women don't wear it—it's like she's gotta announce it to everyone. *(Beat.)* I'm going to ask.

JAYANTI. Don't.

SANGITA. Why not?

JAYANTI.	SANGITA.
She's my roommate, we get along, there's no reason to make things more complicated—	And there's no reason for a woman in the 21st century to cover herself up like that. I bet her father makes her do it.

JAYANTI. No—I've met him—he's very nice. You don't know what— *(SHAMA's prayers end. JAYANTI continues, louder.)* Shama! Como esta? We got you coffee. I hope you like it con lechon. How's my Spanish?

SHAMA *(laughing)*. Very good. Except you asked me if I liked SUCKLING PIG in my coffee.

JAYANTI. I did? What's the word for "milk"?

SANGITA. Con LECHE. Not "lechon."

JAYANTI. Oops. Well. I was close. My Spanish sucks— which is why we're pulling an all-nighter.

SANGITA. No, that's why YOU'RE pulling an all-nighter. Shama and I aren't flunking Spanish—you are.

JAYANTI. I'm not flunking. Exactly. I just don't have the time to study.

SANGITA *(laughing)*. Whatever.

JAYANTI. Come on, it's true. Last quarter I had rehearsals every night for the Mohini project, and this quarter I'm working more hours at the Vedanta Center.

SHAMA. I loved that play. You were great. Como te llamas?

JAYANTI *(begrudgingly)*. Mi nombre es Jayanti.

SHAMA. Encantada.

SANGITA *(to SHAMA)*. Por que usas el hijab?

SHAMA. Que?

JAYANTI. English please!

SANGITA. I thought you can take it off when there aren't men around.

JAYANTI. Sangita…

SANGITA. I want to know!

SHAMA. It's OK. Usually I do take it off when I come home. But tonight I don't want to… This incredible thing happened today. I'm hanging out at Kerckhoff and one of my friends—she's not Muslim—she tells me she likes the hijab I'm wearing, she wants to know where I got it…and this woman comes up to us and says, "Excuse me. I couldn't help but overhear you. Are you Muslim?" I say, "yeah"—not sure what she's getting at…and then she asks me, "What does it look like? What does your hijab look like?" *(Beat.)* The woman was blind. I didn't even know. She holds out her hands and touches my face, touches my scarf, she's asking about the color—she wants to know the EXACT color, she's smiling and nodding. And then she says: "Assalamu Alaikum."

SANGITA. What's that?

JAYANTI. It's Arabic. It means, "Peace be with you."

SHAMA. And then she just walked away.

JAYANTI. Wow.

SANGITA. She was really blind?

SHAMA. It was kinda weird. But it was beautiful too.

JAYANTI. So why DO you wear it?

SHAMA. It's my duty. I believe it's my duty.

SANGITA. To your father?

SHAMA. No—to God. Covering the head is something commanded by God—not Man. And not MEN. That's a stereotype, you know, that men make us wear the scarf.

SANGITA. But it can seem like a stereotype that you wear it. I'm sorry but it makes you look weak.

JAYANTI. Sangita—

SANGITA. It does!

SHAMA. But I became stronger AFTER I put on the scarf. I became ME. Before, I was so caught up in the hair and make-up thing. I was so worried about how I looked.

JAYANTI. But as a woman—I mean, you're a strong woman—

SHAMA. And I'm stronger because I wear the hijab. I think it's more of a feminist statement to put ON the scarf.

SANGITA. Oh come on—

SHAMA. I mean it! It forces me to be in touch with myself as a woman.

SANGITA. By covering yourself up? It's like you're hiding something.

SHAMA.	JAYANTI.
It's not hiding—it's protection.	
There's a difference.	Protection from what though?

SHAMA. When I wear the scarf, people don't treat me like an object. People treat me different.

SANGITA. Maybe they're afraid of you.

SHAMA *(laughing)*. Afraid of ME?

SANGITA. Yeah. Afraid they'll do the wrong thing.

JAYANTI. I feel that way sometimes with you—afraid I might offend you.

SHAMA.	JAYANTI.
But it doesn't have anything to do with you. It's my choice, it's personal.	We're roommates! That doesn't mean it doesn't make me uncomfortable.

SHAMA. DOES it make you uncomfortable?

JAYANTI. No. Well—yeah. Sometimes. I guess. *(To SANGITA.)* This is why I didn't want you to bring it up.

SHAMA. I'm not wearing it for YOUR comfort. *(Beat.)* I'm sorry. That came out wrong. *(Beat.)* Sometimes I don't want to always be the one who's different, you know. Sometimes I want to take it off for one day and just go to the mall and blend in and—

JAYANTI. Let's just drop it.

(JAYANTI turns on a radio/CD player. It's a contemporary pop song. Suddenly TAMEEM bursts into the room. He is a man in his mid-20s. Something is wrong—TAMEEM's face is bloodied, his clothes ripped. He's obviously been in a fight.)

SHAMA.	TAMEEM.
Tameem! What happened?!? Are you all right? Tameem? Jayanti—get a towel	I didn't see them coming—

SANGITA. I'll see if I can find some ice. *(SANGITA exits the room quickly; SHAMA tends to TAMEEM; JAYANTI comes out of the bathroom with a wet towel—the two women dabbing at the blood.)*

SHAMA. Tell me what happened.

TAMEEM. I told you, I didn't see them coming! They came from behind, I think there were three of them.

SHAMA. Why? What did you do?

TAMEEM. They called me Osama. And then they started hitting me.

SHAMA. Oh, Tameem…

(SANGITA rushes back in.)

SANGITA. I found some ice. *(To TAMEEM.)* Hi.

TAMEEM. Hi.

JAYANTI. This is Tameem—Shama's brother.

SANGITA. Hey.

TAMEEM *(to SHAMA)*. There's no reason to tell Mom and Dad.

SHAMA. What do you mean?

TAMEEM *(urgent)*. Promise me.

(SHAMA doesn't answer. The pop song on the radio gets louder and louder and louder. Then blackout.)

SCENE NINE: "The Secret"
Muslim / Glbt

(West Hollywood. A neighborhood park. Afternoon. Several people move in and out of the park. People with dogs, people with baby carriages, runners, old people with caretakers, maybe a bicyclist and a lone skateboarder or two. It's America. And TAMEEM [the brother from the previous scene] sits on a park bench with CONNIE, a woman in her late 30s. They watch the people passing by. TAMEEM's face is badly bruised, there is evidence of scrapes and scratches, a big bandage. He

looks terrible. Some time has passed since the last scene,
but not much. They don't say anything for a while.)

CONNIE. You sure you're OK?

TAMEEM *(shrugs)*. I don't know. But if I'm not, I will be.
Right? *(Beat.)* You know, since 9/11—I've been so
afraid of being Muslim, I guess I forgot to be afraid of
being gay. "Faggot Osama"—that's what they called me,
over and over again.

CONNIE. I'm sorry, Tameem. It's so unfair.

TAMEEM. Do you know what I said? One of them's right
in my face—his eyes, so close—could have been anybody. He punches me again and all I can think to say is:
"Assalamu Alaikum"—"Peace be with you." How crazy
is that? *(Beat.)* I don't know what's worse—that I got
beat up for being gay, or that I told my family it was because I'm Muslim.

CONNIE. Maybe you should tell them the truth.

TAMEEM. I can't.

CONNIE. Tell them what really happened. You're their
son, they love you—

TAMEEM. No—

CONNIE. They might surprise you—

TAMEEM. They won't.

CONNIE. You've talked about wanting to come out to
them for months—

TAMEEM *(laughing, sort of...)*. OK. Let's see—I'll come
out to my family on Monday, after dinner and evening
prayers but before "Queer Eye for the Straight Guy."
(Beat.) I know you're trying to help me, Connie. But
you're not Muslim—you can't understand.

CONNIE. Maybe not. *(Beat.)* I'm not saying it's easy, Tameem. I'm not even really telling you what to do. When I came out to my mother, it was on the phone, and I told her that I'm gay. And without missing a beat she told me that I was working too hard, that maybe all I needed was a little pampering at a beauty salon.

TAMEEM. What did you say?

CONNIE. I was too mad to say anything—hard to believe, I know, but I was speechless. I was mad for days, finally called her up and TOLD her that I'd been mad for days! And she didn't know why—which just made me madder. I said, "Mama! I told you I'm gay and all you could say was that I should go to a beauty salon???" There was this long silence on the phone, and finally my mother, she said, "Connie, I thought you said you were GRAY. You're so young, I couldn't understand why you were going prematurely gray..."

TAMEEM. For real? *(CONNIE and TAMEEM laugh.)*

CONNIE. Mama. She has Alzheimer's now—sometimes she doesn't remember who I am. But she can still say Brucha over the candles. She's not gone yet, but I miss her. *(Beat.)* People can surprise you, Tameem. That's all I'm saying.

TAMEEM. Last week a guy my father works with—a Muslim—he was picked up, whisked away—disappeared. In Los Angeles. For my father, there are more pressing things right now than arguing with me about the finer points of the Koran on homosexuality. Why cause him more pain?

CONNIE. What about your pain? *(TAMEEM looks at CONNIE, doesn't answer. CONNIE waves to a woman coming toward them.)* There they are. Joy! We're over here!

(JOY walks toward them. She's carrying a baby in a pack on her back and a diaper bag. JOY greets both CONNIE and TAMEEM with kisses.)

JOY. Hi. Hi. Sorry we're late. I was already out the door and realized I'd forgotten extra Huggies.

CONNIE *(takes the baby out of the pack, cooing and kissing him)*. Hey, buster. Come to Mommy.

TAMEEM. Wow—he's really grown.

CONNIE. In a week? Really?

TAMEEM. Definitely. Look at him! So beautiful. *(To the baby.)* Hey, Noah...

JOY. And he's really smart too. Just watch the way he watches you. You KNOW he's thinking about stuff. The only thing not cool about him is that he likes listening to Bruce Springsteen.

CONNIE *(to the baby)*. You and your mommy have good taste, don't we? *(To TAMEEM.)* You want to hold him?

TAMEEM. I don't know, I feel kinda like Frankenstein, I'm afraid he might get scared, the way I look.

JOY. I still think you should have filed a police report.

CONNIE. Joy—

JOY. Well it's a CRIME! They were CRIMINALS.

TAMEEM. I know. But it was confusing. And my sister's roommate was there, and I just couldn't— *(Beat.)* The truth is—I'm afraid, you know? *(Beat.)* Every day, more and more, I'm afraid that I'm going to have to choose between being Muslim and being gay.

JOY. Choose? You think you choose to be gay?

TAMEEM. No! But I think I choose to be a practicing homosexual.

CONNIE.	JOY.
As opposed to what—being a monk???	Practicing???
Tameem—	What are you practicing? You practice basketball and the school play—you don't practice being gay.

TAMEEM. We've been through this, Joy.

JOY. Then why are you talking like this? Practicing? *(JOY grabs TAMEEM and hugs him hard.)*

TAMEEM. I'm just trying to—put myself together. I mean— *(Beat.)* Out here, as long as I don't think of myself as being Muslim, I feel OK. Then I visit my family or go to the mosque and as long as I don't think of myself as being GAY—I feel OK. So I never really feel "OK" about any of it.

CONNIE. You can't let them take away your soul, Tameem.

TAMEEM. I'm not just talking about the Muslim community—I don't feel that accepted by the gay community either.

JOY. What about David? Isn't he being supportive? *(There's a long pause.)*

CONNIE. Well? Is he?

TAMEEM. David doesn't know.

JOY.	CONNIE.
What?	David doesn't know you got attacked?

TAMEEM. We split up weeks ago.

CONNIE *(surprised)*.   TAMEEM.
Why?   I was going to tell you and—
                                         (Beat.)

TAMEEM. We went to meet his parents. It was a really big deal for me. They were very liberal, David assured me. He's been out to them since he was in high school. But dinner was awkward, I thought it was just me, you know—I've never met a guy's family like that, I mean as a couple. But the next day, David told me that his parents didn't have a problem with him having a boyfriend—their problem was that his boyfriend was Muslim. So we decided to cool things off for a while. Translation: he dumped me.

JOY. Well he should've dumped his parents, not you! I never liked him anyway. *(CONNIE gives JOY "the look.")* OK, OK, I liked him. But I don't like the way he treated you. It's not cool. *(Beat.)*

TAMEEM. I tried to tell my oldest brother the truth, about what happened— I didn't get very far. I just brought up homosexuality in general and he said that nobody is BORN homosexual—just like nobody is born a thief or a liar or a murderer.

CONNIE. So your brother is an asshole—

TAMEEM. No—he isn't, Connie. It would be so convenient to just hate him—but I don't. He's smart, he's articulate, he's—

CONNIE. Intolerant.

TAMEEM. He is—but he doesn't see it that way. He'd say that just because he doesn't agree with something doesn't make him intolerant.

JOY. What about homophobic?

TAMEEM. He's Muslim—it's what he believes.

JOY. Why are you defending him?

TAMEEM. You don't get it: being gay is still punishable by death in Saudi Arabia—

JOY. And it's illegal to have sex in Georgia with the lights on!

CONNIE. Joy, you're not helping.

JOY *(frustrated)*. Maybe not. But this whole religious thing—I don't get it! I mean, I thought religion was supposed to be a GOOD thing. Seems like it just causes a lot of pain. It's messed up.

CONNIE. It's not the religion—it's the people who are messed up.

JOY. Well the people ARE the religion. And given how much they all seem to hate gay people—Catholics, Christians, Muslims—you can have your religion. You can have all of it.

CONNIE. I don't want all of it. I just want the good parts.

TAMEEM. That's not how it works.

CONNIE. I know, you're right. *(To JOY.)* You're right.

TAMEEM *(to CONNIE)*. Why are you Jewish?

CONNIE *(thinking)*. Why am I Jewish...why did Moses cross the Red Sea?

TAMEEM. To get to other side?

CONNIE *(laughing)*. Kind of. Growing up, being Jewish was mostly cultural. But getting older, after my divorce, after coming out—I wanted more. I wanted to KNOW more. Was Judaism rejecting me...or was I rejecting Judaism? And if I was going to CHOOSE to reject Judaism, then I wanted to know what I was rejecting. The funny part—after all of my searching, all of my looking at other religions, going to different services, trying to find where I fit in, all of my questions, all of my anger…I realized that even if I did reject Judaism, even if I could—I'm still Jewish. *(Beat.)* Why am I Jewish? Why am I a lesbian? It's who I am. *(TAMEEM nods, understands.)*

JOY. OK. You're Jewish, you can't live with it, you can't live without it. Fine. But here's what I don't get: it's just one more institution run by a bunch of sexist men who've done nothing but take money from poor people and degrade women for centuries.

CONNIE *(to TAMEEM)*. We avoid this subject whenever possible. It's gotten harder since Noah was born.

JOY. Connie wants to raise Noah Jewish.

CONNIE. We talked about this while I was pregnant—

JOY. But now he's here, he's with us! And raising him in a religion—in any religion—it just feels like child abuse to me. Like brainwashing.

CONNIE. I want my son—our son to grow up with a sense of identity—of Jewish identity. And part of the reason is because if he doesn't—it's going to be that much harder for him not to get sucked into Christianity. OK. I said it. But it's true! Christianity is always hanging around, it's always waiting at the door. Always, always, always.

TAMEEM. Did you grow up in a religion?

JOY. No, I grew up in a family. We didn't talk about religion, it wasn't important. I remember one time, I was little, maybe nine or ten. I was watching TV. I remember I was watching "The Wonder Years." And my mom was doing the ironing. She suddenly looked up and said to me, "If anybody ever tells you you have to go to church—try to get them to take you to the Unitarian church. The Unitarians don't seem to talk about God as much." And then she went back to ironing.

CONNIE. For a while I tried to ignore God, just calling myself "spiritual." But it felt so wishy-washy. It wasn't enough. Sometimes I get angry with God—but I refuse to abandon Her. I think—it's harder to leave a religion than it is to fall in love with one. Falling in love—that's the easy part…it's STAYING in love that can drive you crazy.

JOY *(teasing)*. Amen. *(JOY kisses CONNIE.)*

TAMEEM. That's how it is for me. I can't give up on it. I know that Allah loves His creations—and I'm one of His creations. I mean, if Allah has given me this soul—this GAY soul—then how can I not love it? And how can He not love me? I can't just be part of myself—part Muslim, part gay, part son, part brother, part lover—I want to put all of those things together. I want to be ALL of me. I want to figure this out. *(Frustrated/exhausted.)* Why can't I figure this out???

CONNIE. You will.

JOY. Or you won't.

CONNIE. You just have to go through it.

(A woman [MICHELLE] approaches, handing out flyers.)

MICHELLE. Hi. Sorry to interrupt—but I was wondering if I can leave a flyer with you.

CONNIE. Sure.

JOY. What's it for?

MICHELLE *(handing JOY a flyer)*. There's going to be a rally on Saturday to protest any more development of the wetlands in Playa Vista.

CONNIE. Thanks.

MICHELLE. Please come if you can. *(MICHELLE continues on her way.)*

CONNIE. What's it say? *(JOY shows CONNIE and TAMEEM the flyer, they all read it to themselves.)*

TAMEEM. Wow.

CONNIE. Maybe we should go. *(They watch people going by. To TAMEEM:)* Your turn to hold Noah.

TAMEEM. You sure?

CONNIE. He's asleep. You'll be surprised how calming it is…it gives you perspective. *(CONNIE gently puts the baby in TAMEEM's arms.)* Holding him, just listening to him breathe. It's the sound of praying.

JOY. It's the sound of love.

TAMEEM. It's the sound of perfection. *(The baby stirs, fusses. TAMEEM tries to hand the baby to CONNIE.)*

CONNIE *(laughing)*. You're on your own.

JOY. You just have to go through it.

TAMEEM *(looks down at the baby)*. Hey, Noah. Shhhhhh. *(JOY and CONNIE watch TAMEEM as he gently leans in and kisses the baby.)*

JOY. There's the family you're born into—and the one that you make. *(Without looking at each other, CONNIE and JOY touch hands. TAMEEM looks lovingly at the two women.)*

TAMEEM. And maybe there's the one that's both.

CONNIE. What do you mean?

TAMEEM. I'm gonna tell my sister.

(CONNIE looks at him, nods. People walk/run/ride by. Hardly anyone gives a second look at the little family sitting on the park bench. The lights slowly shift: JULIA

[the ESL teacher from Scene One] stands in a single pool of light talking on her cell phone:)

JULIA *(on cell phone)*. Hello? Yes, this is Julia. Who is this? *(Beat.)* Oh, God. Yes. Right. I know. OK. What day do you need me to be there? OK. *(Firm.)* I'll be there. No but I can Mapquest it. Yeah I know that area—I teach at a Catholic church in Long Beach. I teach English. No—the language. ESL, right. I'm really an actress. Do I need to bring anything? Right. Wait— can I ask—how many are there, how many did they find? *(She listens to the answer, long pause.)* No—I'm still here. I'll be there.

(JULIA walks right into the next scene. The last actor sitting in the 48 chairs stands. It is JESUS. He sheds his costume from the Pilgrimage Play.*)*

SCENE TEN: "Jesus of Los Angeles"
Glbt / Tongva

(Playa Vista. Archeological dig. Telltale signs of real estate development. Day. JULIA looks around, unsure what she's supposed to do. JESUS—a Latino in his 30s—approaches JULIA.)

JESUS. Hi. Are you Julia?
JULIA *(nervous)*. Yeah, yes. I'm Julia. Hi.
JESUS. I'm Jesus. We talked on the phone.
JULIA. Right! Jesus. Thank you. Well. I made it.
JESUS. I'm glad.

JULIA. I'm a little nervous. I've never done this, anything like this.

JESUS. I understand. We really appreciate you being here.

JULIA. So how does it work? What, what do I do? How can I help?

JESUS. You're here. That's the most important thing. We're here to watch, just to monitor. After a burial site is discovered, there's a procedure that's supposed to be followed. We're here to make sure that happens. *(JULIA nods.)* Sure you're OK? *(JULIA nods, watches as a few people delicately lift a bone out of the ground and carefully place it in heavy fabric.)* I know—it's intense.

JULIA. Ninety-two bodies. Bones. It's unbelievably sad to watch your ancestors being dug up, especially when you believe the land is sacred—this place was chosen as a burial site for a sacred reason.

JESUS. Are you Tongva?

JULIA *(nodding)*. Half. Yeah. Like a cake mix… My mother's family is Tongva. I'm still learning about it. I don't know a whole lot of the history, bits and pieces.

JESUS. Cahuenga. Cucamonga. Topanga. Azusa. Those places are all Tongva words. *(Beat.)*

JULIA. It's more quiet than I thought it would be. It feels like… *(Her voice trails off.)*

JESUS. Church? *(Agreeing.)* It's holy. Sacred. *(They are both quiet, like a moment of prayer. Then:)*

JULIA. Last night I had this dream, I dreamed that I was here, that I was here watching them dig up the burial site…and they pulled out bones—and I knew that the bones were my family. And I was trying to put them together, you know, trying to reconstruct—something. These bones, they fit together like a jigsaw puzzle…and they stood up, like a person. And the bones started to move, to dance. And—and— *(Realization:)* it was me. The bones were me. I had put myself together. Or tried to. *(Beat.)* Do you know if you run spell-check on my computer—the word "Tongva" shows up as a misspelled word. It doesn't even exist. *(Shrugs.)* Wow. I'm here. *(Beat.)* How about you? How did you get involved?

JESUS. Oh I've been an activist for a long time. I've found that in the Native American culture, people and things that are different aren't diminished, sometimes they're even considered more special.

JULIA. What do you mean?

JESUS. The word "transgender" doesn't exist in spell-check either. *(JESUS moves quickly downstage, watching them lifting bones from the ground. Then:)* They would never dig up Forest Lawn like this. *(Beat.)* I know what it means to have to dig, to uncover parts of yourself that most people don't realize are there. To lift them up.

JULIA. You're…?

JESUS. I'm from a little place in the desert. Middle of nowhere if you're not from around there. But the middle of the universe if it's the only thing you know. When I was born my parents named me Maria de los Angeles—no pressure, right? *(Laughing.)* I was very religious as a kid. I loved going to church, I loved it! I loved hearing stories from the Bible. It was the story of the resurrection that got me the most. I don't know if I thought it was true—the part where Jesus came back to life—but something about that story had meaning for me—it still does. By the time I was fourteen, I was dying inside. I was just a bunch of bones dancing around—like in your dream. But inside, INSIDE I was dead. I couldn't talk to anyone in our church about it. When people said, "I don't understand that girl"—what they really meant was "If I don't understand—then I can't approve." For me, there was no one else to talk to—except God. So I talked to God all the time... There's a difference between talking and praying, you know. Praying, you have the feeling there are millions of prayers being said at the same time and it's like you're waiting at the end of a long line, or on hold with bad muzak playing. But when you TALK to God—you get him right away. It's just him and you. And it was during those talks that I figured out that I had to have my own kind of resurrection. So I left, I left that little place in the desert...and I came to Los Angeles—barely eighteen. After years of hanging on a cross—I resurrected. Maria de los Angeles became Jesus.

JULIA. Jesus of Los Angeles.

JESUS. After a couple of years, I was missing my family so much. I loved them, I wanted to see them. But most of all: I wanted them to see ME, to love ME, the real me. I called and told them I wanted to come back to visit. I told them my name is Jesus now. My mom told me she loved me... *"ti quiero, ti quiero y regresa a casa, mi amore."* She told me to come home. *(Beat.)* When I left, I was their daughter. When I returned, I was their son. But I wasn't a different person—I was just more, MORE of the SAME person. When I went back, there was this huge sign on my parents' front porch. It said, "Welcome Home, Jesus de Los Angeles!" They were all there, all of my family, every one of them, it was a big party. And at that moment I saw my family break with religion, they crossed that line to support me. It was like God opening the windows and letting in so much light. *(Quiet.)*

JULIA. Thank you.

JESUS. It's this place, I guess. It's your ancestors. There's something about it that makes you tell the truth.

JULIA. My mother says that the most disgraceful thing a Tongva can do—is to fail to show courage. *(A CELL PHONE RINGS—piercing the mood.)* Oh God. Sorry. I'll turn it off.

JESUS. No—you should always answer the call. You never know if it'll ring again.

(JULIA walks upstage to talk on the cell phone. We cannot hear her conversation. JESUS looks out at the burial site. ALL OF THE CAST begin to re-enter in silence, watching JULIA on the phone. JULIA hangs up the phone and turns to face JESUS. She is shaken.)

JESUS *(cont'd)*. Are you OK?

JULIA *(stunned)*. I got this role that I had to read for like five times. It's a play—it's a big role.

JESUS. Wow, amazing. Congratulations.

JULIA. No—I haven't told you the amazing part yet. The character is a Tongva woman. I'm going to play a Tongva.

JESUS. Do you have a lot of lines?

JULIA. Uh-huh. And they're all in Tongva— *(Overwhelmed.)* I'm finally going to learn the language!

(The TONGVA ELDER from the prologue appears upstage in the hillside:)

TONGVA ELDER. Well it's about time. *(To the audience.)* I was raised Catholic...but I AM Tongva-Gabrielino. What are you?

(Spread out all over the theater, all of the cast members step forward and say, "I am Catholic," "I am a born-again Hindu," "I am an ardent atheist," "I am a Jew from Buffalo," "I was raised straight," "I was raised Catholic but played a Buddhist," etc.,—the actor's true personal relationship to faith. These overlap and build to a loud... Silence. Then MRS. STEVENSON takes her place center stage—right where she belongs.)

MRS. STEVENSON. Well. *(MRS. STEVENSON looks out at the audience, searching, connecting. Moved/perplexed/envious.)* What a time you live in. *(Beat.)* Good night, dears—and thank you for coming.

(The lights slowly fade to black and...)

THE PLAY IS OVER

PLAYWRIGHT'S ACKNOWLEDGEMENTS:

— Dozens and dozens of interviews, potluck lunches, community dialogues, story circles with community partners and Cornerstone ensemble members.

— Rehearsals and productions of all of the plays and projects in Cornerstone's Faith-Based Theater Cycle.

— The character ShahAb's letter home from Iraq, inspired by actual letters written by American soldiers from the Iraq War, in particular: Army Staff Sgt. Dale Panchot of Northome, Minn.; and Army Pfc. Rachel K. Bosveld of Oshkosh, Wis.

— The Tongva website: www.tongvatribe.com

— A sermon by the Pastor Jeff Miner of the Jesus Metropolitan Community Church (Carmel, Ind.).

— *The Pilgrimage Play* originally dramatized by Christine Wetherill Stevenson. Text at the beginning of my play comes directly from Mrs. Stevenson's play.

— Mrs. Christine Wetherill Stevenson biographical information based on information from the John Anson Ford website; theatermania.com; KCET transcripts; American Magazine (April 1926); Ancestry.com; Los Angeles Times.

— Diana Gish. Gary Glickman. Rich Cooper. Janet Allen. Joel Grynheim. Juan Ramirez.

— Special thanks to Elizabeth Gonzalez, Nathaniel Justiniano, Ann-Sophie Morrisette, Emily Golding and Shaunda Miles who tirelessly arranged all of my community activities for more than three years.

— The original 57-member cast and design team LONG BRIDGE... every one of you taught me something.

— Scott Horstein for talking me down from the ledge several times.

— Bill Rauch for believing I could write this. Even now. Especially now.

— And to the literally dozens of total strangers these past three years who have sat next to me in coffee shops and on airplanes and buses and subways...and mysteriously began talking to me about religion. I have no idea how you knew I needed to know—but I'm grateful.

What a time we live in.

— James Still

DIRECTOR'S NOTES